Money, Social Ontology and Law

T0318223

Presenting legal and philosophical essays on money, this book explores the conditions according to which an object like a piece of paper, or an electronic signal, has come to be seen as having a value.

Money plays a crucial role in the regulation of social relationships and their normative determination. It is thus integral to the very nature of the "social", and the question of how society is kept together by a network of agreements, conventions, exchanges, and codes. All of which must be traced down. The technologies of money discussed here by Searle, Ferraris, and Condello show how we conceive the category of the social at the intersection of individual and collective intentionality, documentality, and materiality. All of these dimensions, as the introduction to this volume demonstrates, are of vital importance for legal theory and for a whole set of legal concepts that are crucial in reflections on the relationship between law, philosophy, and society.

Angela Condello, University of Torino

Maurizio Ferraris, University of Torino

John Rogers Searle, University of California, Berkeley

Part of the Law and Politics: Continental Perspectives series
Series editors: Mariano Croce
Sapienza University of Rome, Italy

Marco Goldoni
University of Glasgow, UK

For information about the series and details of previous and forthcoming titles, see www.routledge.com/law/series/LPCP

Money, Social Ontology and Law

Angela Condello, Maurizio Ferraris and John Rogers Searle

Routledge
Taylor & Francis Group
a GlassHouse Book

First published 2019
by Routledge
2 Park Square, Milton Park, Abingdon, Oxon OX14 4RN

and by Routledge
52 Vanderbilt Avenue, New York, NY 10017

First issued in paperback 2020

A GlassHouse book

Routledge is an imprint of the Taylor & Francis Group, an informa business

British Library Cataloguing-in-Publication Data
A catalogue record for this book is available from the British Library

Library of Congress Cataloging-in-Publication Data
Names: Searle, John R., contributor. | Ferraris, Maurizio, 1956- ,
    contributor. | Condello, Angela, 1984- , contributor, editor.
Title: Money, social ontology and law / by John Rogers Searle and
    Maurizio Ferraris ; edited by Angela Condello.
Description: Abingdon, Oxon ; New York, NY : Routledge, 2019. | Series:
    Law and politics: continental perspectives | Includes bibliographical
    references.
Identifiers: LCCN 2019001903 (print) | LCCN 2019009503
    (ebook) | ISBN 9780429200526 (ebk) | ISBN 9780367191115 (hbk)
Subjects: LCSH: Money—Social aspects. | Money—Philosophy. |
    Economics—Sociological aspects.
Classification: LCC HG221 (ebook) | LCC HG221 .M81425 2019
    (print) | DDC 306.3/4—dc23LC record available at https://lccn.
    loc.gov/2019001903

ISBN 13: 978-0-367-67179-2 (pbk)
ISBN 13: 978-0-367-19111-5 (hbk)

Typeset in Times New Roman
by Apex CoVantage, LLC

Contents

Acknowledgments

The authors are very grateful to Einaudi, and in particular to Andrea Bosco, who first proposed and promoted the publication of *Il denaro e i suoi inganni*. They are also thankful to Mariano Croce and Marco Goldoni, who direct the Routledge series "Law and Politics: Continental Perspectives". And, equally, to Colin Perrin.

Introduction

Angela Condello

1. Why *a* book on money?

Since antiquity, human beings have wondered about money and about how it works. Money is everywhere and it is likely to be among the most recurrent and continuous elements (and instruments) in human civilization, together with law: it has been present through centuries. Still, it remains (if possible) even more mysterious than law. There are theories that explain how its value is determined, but if we look at a simple object like a coin or a banknote as such, we will all agree that it is nothing *in* and *of* itself. Undoubtedly, coins are not made of precious metals and banknotes are pieces of paper with encrypted print. Yet, even in a globalized and digital economy, it would be hard to name a thing more central than money. Money lies at the core of human bonds, and it symbolizes exchange. Always, and everywhere.

Against these premises, then, why *a* (or, worse: *another*) book on money, today? The answer is quite obvious: precisely because, despite the radical changes that our society is going through – first and foremost the dominant authority of digital technologies – money continues to function as a *unit of measurement*. It is a point of reference of every societal theory. It continues to exist despite the paradigm shifts: it just measures other, new, and different social objects as well as other, new, and different forms of human relations. This book *starts* from money, then, in order to use it as a filter, as a key to interpret the continuities and discontinuities that characterize human civilization when observed from the perspective of theoretical and legal philosophy. Moreover, this book situates money at the center of all societal meanings and it concludes by attributing to it the capacity to represent a *symbol* of societal exchange, of all trades: in some sense, money emerges as a material metaphor of the role played by language in the construction of social reality. It does so by bringing the attention back to a device that is changing radically in its form, but not in the essence. As a matter of fact, one could object that bitcoin could constitute a brand new and different form of money. And, to some extent, they are. Nevertheless, we shall see how the core structure of money, even (and perhaps especially) with bitcoin, remains the same. From bags of salt, to shells, to talismans, until coins, banknotes, and bitcoin: the essence of money reveals the essence of human society, or – to use Searle's words – of *human civilization.*

2. Why *this* book on money?

John Searle and Maurizio Ferraris have been debating on social ontology, and more specifically on money, for a couple of years now. Both internationally renowned philosophers, they have developed their careers in different spatial, intellectual, and temporal environments. Searle studied in Oxford during the sixties, and became a disciple of Austin and Strawson – his social ontology stems from the idea that, through the performative force of speech acts, we create institutions. And we also attribute value to them, as it is in the case of money, that was not "created" from nothing, but started gaining a certain value and power in time.

Ferraris grew up, intellectually, in continental Europe, a disciple and then colleague and friend of Jacques Derrida. For him, there would be no social reality without the power of recording. Their complementary and concurrently opponent theories on social ontology have found in money the ideal site for confrontation. It is no surprise, then, that when first discussing a book on money with Maurizio Ferraris, and thus when first presented with the possibility of going back to the basic structure of his social ontology, John Searle confessed that he was very excited about it. With hindsight, I would say that he was excited for two main reasons. Firstly, because he would have one more chance to affirm his theory of intentionality against opponent theories: as a matter of fact, money had already been – for decades – among his favorite examples. We thus envisaged to construct this project as a confrontation, or an imaginary dialogue, between the two philosophers. Searle was pretty excited, as I said, and so was Ferraris, for the same (and opposite) reason. Secondly, because he had never reflected on money, and yet he had recently reached the conclusion that the example of money was present everywhere in his books. The original project was published in 2018, in Italian, under the title *Il denaro e i suoi inganni,* by Einaudi.

After the publication, the debate between the two kept growing; then, the original conclusive essay (in the Italian version) I added to their chapters opened the field of this work to another symbolic language – law – by building a parallel between these two paradigmatic social "technologies". In the present monograph, I develop the part on legal ontology by showing how the paradigmatic socio-legal object, money, performs its phenomenology in the frame of a complex space – at the intersection of various languages and realms – to the extent that it invites others to develop some reflections on the plural realms involved by its symbolic value and function, in a sort of Lacanian circularity or *regressus ad infinitum*.

3. Money, social ontology, and law

Why *this* book on money, then? Because Searle's and Ferraris's perspectives allow us to situate money among the broader field of social ontology and thus show its crucial importance for a thorough understanding of society.

Social ontology is the branch of philosophy that aims at analyzing the structures of the social world so it engages with all its components: (*a*) social agents, individuals, or collective agents; (*b*) organized groups; (*c*) their actions and beliefs; (*d*) the social objects, like contracts, marriages, institutions, abstractions such as the president of the Italian Republic (so: all those objects that are not natural objects and that do not exist independently of human actions). Social ontology is thus particularly focused on the distinction between the natural world and those dimensions of reality that are constructed artificially, such as – for instance – law, economics, exchanges, money. These do not exist independently of human activity. The threshold between these two dimensions – natural, institutional – is at the core of all questions addressed by social ontologists and it is from this perspective that the imaginary debate between Searle and Ferraris contained in this book must be considered. The background question behind this work is: "What are the conditions that allow us to consider a piece of paper as money?" In my chapter, I try to argue that this question is similar to a basic question of legal theory and namely: "What are the conditions that allow us to consider a series of propositions as law? What attributes normativity to such propositions?"

So, again, why *this* book on money? As aforementioned, the works on this subject are many, both in human and social sciences. Among all, I would certainly mention Georg Simmel's *The Philosophy of Money* (1900) and Marcel Mauss's *The Gift* (1925) as traditional and fundamental works on the origins, the functions, and the phenomenology of exchange and of money. Then, for decades, the topic has seemed to be the intellectual territory of economists and mathematicians. Recently (2016), philosopher of economics and society Francesco Guala has made the important effort to position the theory of money among other institutions, following social ontologists such as John Rogers Searle, who never before the publication of the chapter contained in the present book – which reproduces an article originally published in 2017 by the *Cambridge Journal of Economics* – had openly engaged with a work on money. Although money has always been among his favorite examples, in fact, this is the first time that Searle elaborates his own theory of money. Unlike traditional works on money, this book presents a new, different perspective on the topic, since it aims at showing the conditions that make us believe that an object like a piece of paper, or an electronic signal, has a value (that is partly dependent on the observer, and partly not). It does so through a triple perspective: an ontology of money (Searle), a metaphysics of money as a technology which mediates between reality and what we know about it (Ferraris), and the attempt to bridge these theories of money with a larger field of questions relevant for social scientists.

Money is the cornerstone of oppositions like concretion and abstraction, personal and impersonal, and thus concerns human relationships and the function played by the regulation of those relationships. As suggested by Georg Simmel, money shows the surface level of economic and human affairs, and it touches upon those fortuitous phenomena that characterize the life of humankind within a regulated society. It shows the relation of all relations, the one that attributes value to objects: so it shows both the surface and the roots of social exchange and reveals the normative character of such a bond.

Money is the reifier of all relations: it is a tool and *intermediary* of social relations. It thus shows what it means to be "social", what is the ontology of society, and how society is kept together by nets of agreements, conventions, exchanges, codes, and recordings. The "technologies" of money discussed by Searle and Ferraris show how we conceive the category of the social at the intersection of individual and collective intentionality, documentality, and systems of recording, and the material technologies on which these converge.

As observed by Peter Fitzpatrick in a recent contribution about law and society (Mulqueen and Matthews, *Being Social*, Counterpress 2016), within the field of law and society, law is often conceived as an *offspring* of society. Yet, there is another strand in law and society that endows law with distinctness and efficacy of its own, and with some autonomy. The act of engaging with two different and complementary theories about money as a social and institutional object sheds light on the complexity that characterizes legal ontology as well.

Searle believes that social reality (institutions, professional titles, money, property, etc.) is constructed by subjects. In order to exist, something like a $5-dollar banknote must be represented and collectively recognized as valid by a sufficient number of subjects within a community. Ferraris, on the other hand, claims that collective intentionality does not explain the complexity of the social world. In order to understand this world, we must look instead at documents, at recordings, i.e. where the intentionality (of which Searle speaks) is deposited. Without such a system of traces, there would be no social world. In some sense, this work on money suggests an innovative interpretation of social reality in terms of an "intentional grammatology". We could say that Searle explains how language and intentionality mobilize the social world by creating obligations, rights, and possibilities, with the same peremptoriness of physical injunctions. On the other hand, Ferraris retraces the essence of money, which is recording: today, money could be reduced to pure bits on a computer and it reveals an essence which is older than the pyramids. This book presents an exemplary dialogue between an analytic philosopher and a continental philosopher, who are united by a passion for speaking clearly about concrete things.

The final chapter explains why the philosophical theories presented by Searle and Ferraris – though concerning money, more directly – are important to understand the relationship between law and society. In other words, the final chapter positions the whole book within the critical studies on law and society by showing how the two philosophical systems described by Searle and Ferraris concern the social bond, and the existence of social institutions.

One final word about the role of status functions as a bridging theme between the two ontological perspectives presented in the book: Searle concludes that money is a status function, generated by a speech act. In other words, it is something that would not exist without a declaration that makes it valid and valuable. He has stated in many of his works that all institutions are status functions. In a recent interview, I asked Searle about the relationship between speech acts theory and law, and he claimed:[1]

> The promulgations of laws are always types of speech acts, but once promulgated the laws themselves are linguistic representations and thus they fall into the category of speech acts. As far as positive law is concerned, it seems to me that there are two categories. There are laws that are regulative, like "Drive on the right-hand side of a road", and laws that are constitutive, like "We form a corporation that has such and such procedures". Regulative laws regulate the forms of behaviour, and constitutive laws enable us to create new institutional facts, or corporations, and everything that can be created by a legal procedure. This

---

1 See Angela Condello and John Rogers Searle, "Some Remarks About Social Ontology and Law: An Interview With John R. Searle", in *Ratio Juris*, Vol. 30, No. 2, 2017, pp. 226–231, p. 226 in particular.

is how I would roughly describe the interconnections between law and speech act theory: The promulgation of law is a speech act, but once promulgated, the law is itself a speech act and it either regulates an existing form of behaviour (drive on the right) or enables us to create a new form of behaviour like the creation of governments, departments, and so on.

The performative acts that generate status functions can explain why some objects gain a power, or force, or why they come to existence just because it is conventionally stated that they exist – Searle has stated that one of the most remarkable things about humans is that they can create reasons for acting that are independent of their inclinations and desires. In order to explain how this is possible, Searle traces back the origin of these functions to language. Language is what counts for the creation of these deontic powers, like that of law, but also the power we have in case we owe a certain amount of valid banknotes. This book helps focusing on the "intentional" origin of money (Searle), and yet at the same time it questions it (Ferraris). If it was only a matter or a voluntary decision to attribute value to a certain object, then how could we explain financial crises? According to Ferraris, all institutional reality shows that it is a mistake to presuppose something like a "spirit" behind the letter (that is to say, the files, documents, and recordings proving the existence of social institutions).

This monograph brings the focus on the importance that philosophical theories of money have within a broader theory and conceptualization of society, by conclusively bringing the focus on the parallel between the evaluative nature of both money and law.

1 Money

Ontology and deception[1]

John Rogers Searle

I hold in my hand a United States $20 bill. It is, like most things we take for granted, philosophically astounding. (One mark of a philosopher is to be amazed by what any sane person takes for granted.) The bill contains a lot of writing, much of which is the repetition of the number twenty, eight times in numerals and three times in words, "Twenty Dollars" twice and "Twenty" once under a seal. It contains only two sentences: "This note is legal tender for all debts public and private" (How do they know?) and "In God we trust" (What happens to those who do not trust in God? Is it not money for them?). It also contains pictures of Andrew Jackson and the White House, and various seals and serial numbers as well as the words "Federal Reserve Note". "The United States of America" occurs on both sides. This chapter is primarily concerned with the question: What fact or facts make this a piece of paper money? To understand why it is money and what it means to be money you have to understand a whole civilization. I will not explain the whole civilization, but I will explain some of the money part. In writing this text, I discovered a series of deceptions (illusions, systematic falsehoods) in the institution of money, and I will try to identify them.

I also have on my computer screen a photograph of a Confederate $100 bill. It is even more amazing. It says "The Confederate States of America will pay the bearer $100 on demand"; all of that is in large print. But in much smaller boxes on each side of a picture of an unnamed woman, it says, "two years after the ratification of the treaty of peace", then in the next box, "between the Confederate States of America and the United States of America". Though both bills are supposed to function in the same way, as money, their status as speech acts is quite different. The American bill is a Declaration. By Declaration, this piece of paper counts as $20 in the United States.

1 As aforementioned, a version of this text was originally published in the *Cambridge Journal of Economics*, 2017, 41 [doi:10.1093/cje/bex034], pp. 1453–1470, under the same title, "Money: Ontology and Deception".

The Confederate money is a Commissive, a complex conditional promise. It says the government promises to pay the bearer on two conditions: first that there is a ratified treaty of peace between the Confederate States of America in the United States of America, and second that two years have passed since the peace was ratified.

1. The functions of money and the definition of money

What, then, is money? It is not easy to find explicit definitions of "money", but textbook accounts of the function of money, I think, implicitly contain a definition. Money performs two functions, and on some accounts, three. First, money is a medium of exchange. Second, it is a store of value. And third, on some accounts, it is a measure of value. These characterizations are not as clear as they might be, but examples will give them more substance. "I bought this shirt for $20" reports the use of money as a medium of exchange; "I have $1,000 in my bank account" reports the use of money as a store of value; "My car is worth $10,000" reports the use of money as a measure of value.

Are these sufficient to define money? I don't think so. First off, the money when I buy a shirt, is not a "medium" of exchange. It is an object of exchange. So I gave one object, a $20 bill, and I got another object, a shirt. No "medium" was involved. Furthermore, when I buy something, I don't need to give a physical object. With debit cards, for example, you can just transfer money from one account to another with no physical objects actually being exchanged. In order to clarify the definition, we would have to explain what exchange is, and what value is. Exchange is not hard because it involves giving one object for another object, as when I trade my $20 bill for a shirt. With the giving of the objects, deontic powers of ownership are transferred. Value is harder because it involves desire and one can knowingly and consistently hold inconsistent desires in a way one can knowingly and consistently hold inconsistent beliefs. I will not discuss exchange and value further, but assume that we can use both notions. We can take "store" more or less for granted because it is not specifically tied to human civilization. Squirrels store nuts for the winter. Furthermore, this "medium of exchange" talk leaves out one of the most important functions of money, payments where no exchange is made, for example taxes. You have to pay taxes in money, but you get nothing by way of "exchange".

Again, before explaining money, we should note that the textbooks identify three types of money. First, there is *commodity* money. This is the use of a commodity as money. The commodity can be gold, silver, squirrel pelts, seashells, or whatever the community decides. In its simplest form, commodity money is like barter. You trade one type of object for goods and services. Not all trade involves money. If I give you a piece of silver for your shirt, so far no money has changed hands. If pieces of silver or shirts are standardly used for the purposes of such exchanges then they become money for reasons I hope to make clear. Second, there is *contract* money. Here, the object used as money is a contract to pay the bearer such and such on demand. Paradoxically, many such money contracts promise to pay the bearer so much money, as was illustrated by the Confederate $100 bill. How can *money consist in a contract to pay money in return for the contract when the only money you could get would be another contract?* As we will see later, this is one of the common forms of deception involved in money. It still says on British currency, and until fairly recently used to say on US reserve notes, that the Treasury promises to pay the bearer so much money on demand. But of course, in the United States and the United Kingdom there is no such thing as money with which they can pay you in addition to the sort of thing you are holding in your hand when you have the currency. So the promise to pay is, in effect, meaningless because what you would be paid in is exactly what you already have. I will say more about this later. Finally, and most commonly nowadays, there is *fiat* money. Such and such a type of entity is money because some authority, such as the State, declares it to be money by fiat. But now, our puzzlement increases: What facts about these three different kinds make them all money?

One way to answer that question is to tell the story about the evolution of money. The point is not that the story is historically accurate. Presumably it is not, but it illustrates the logical relations. In the beginning, there is only commodity money such as gold and silver, but it is inconvenient to carry gold and silver around, so one leaves it with a man who sits on a bench called a bank. The man is called a banker. In return for the gold and silver, the man gives you a set of documents that constitute promises to pay the bearer in the gold and silver in the bank. This is much more convenient and safer than carrying actual pieces of metal. But as long as the banker honors the contracts, the contracts are as good as gold. The contracts now replace the commodity as money. Another form of flexibility, and a form of deception that is easy and really inevitable, is to issue more contracts than the actual amount of gold and silver in the bank. As long as everybody does not run to the bank all at once, the contracts function just fine. However, for any number of reasons it becomes historically tempting to forget about the gold and silver and just have the "contracts". The story goes that this money then becomes *fiat* money because it is only really money because some authority says it is money. Typically, the old promises are verbally repeated on the fiat money: "The Bank of England promises to pay the bearer on demand ten pounds", but the promises are meaningless because the only thing they can pay you with is what you already have. In the United States, this step is known as "going off the gold standard" and it occurred in two stages: first, in 1933 when the government announced that they would not redeem paper currency in gold to individual citizens, and second, in 1971 when the government announced that they would not provide other governments with gold in return for US dollars. The move from contract money to fiat money is supposed to illustrate how the same functions can be performed even though the underlying ontology is quite different.

The notion of a "fiat" seems to imply an explicit act of performing a fiat. This is not necessarily the case. The point is that something might gradually evolve as money through general *acceptance*. The point, however, is that it will turn out that some assignment of status function is essential to performing the functions of money. This always requires a Declaration whereby some representation makes it the case that it is money. This is normally called a "fiat", and it will turn out that all money, in this sense, is fiat money. The interesting distinction is not between commodity money, contract money, and fiat money but between commodity money, contract money, and what I will call *baseless* money, money which is not backed by anything.

But, if it remains money all along, then we have to ask, what exactly are the functions of money which will serve to define it? What are the functions that money serves?

Here is a list:

1 The possessor can buy goods and services with money. For this reason, money is *power*. The person who has money has more power than the person who does not. The power in question is *deontic*, having to do with rights, obligations, etc. When I have a $20 bill, I have a right to buy things with that money and I have the power to pay my debts up to $20 worth. This will turn out to be the essential feature of money.
2 You can make payments, such as debts, even those that have nothing to do with buying anything. Taxes are an obvious example, but all sorts of transfer payments would be included: payment from parents to children, blackmail, extortion, cash gifts, and countless others.
3 Money is a store of value. Because of 1 and 2, you store something of value when you save your money, either in cash or in a bank account.
4 Money is a measure of value. The question "How much is it worth?" is typically answered by stating a money value.

What else is there? Here, more or less at random and pre-theoretically, are some further features of money that I hope to explain:

5 Money is essentially *social*. There are lots of valuable artifacts that can be used either privately or socially, works of art for example. But

money can only function between people or institutions. Robinson Crusoe, alone on his island, has no use for money. Money requires society and collective intentionality between members of the society. As far as I know, money is unique in that it is believed to be valuable by each individual only on the assumption that everybody else believes it to be valuable, and believes that everybody else believes it to be valuable, and so on up in a potentially infinite, but non-vicious, hierarchy.

6   Money is essentially *digital*. You cannot have an analog form of money because, in order to perform its functions, money has to be countable. You have to be able to give a numerical value to answer such questions as how much the object costs, how much the object is worth, and how much you have saved. Whether squirrel pelts, gold ounces, or dollars, there has to be a numerical answer to the question, how much?

7   Money, when functioning as money, is *not valued for its own sake*. People may use gold as jewelry or tooth fillings, but when used as money its only function is to buy, sell, pay, store, and measure. Its possession is always a means to an end, not an end in itself.

8   Money has to be *exchangeable or transferable*. It is essential to the functioning of money that quantities of money must be transferable from one agent to another. It is easy to see that this is essential for money to perform its functions as an object of exchange. It is said that at some points in ancient Sparta money consisted of huge iron bars because the authorities did not want money to be taken out of town. So the transfer need not involve a movable physical movement, but it must involve a recognizable transfer of rights. If a community uses mountains as money, then paying with a mountain must involve a transfer of the right to use the mountain as money from the payer to the payee.

9   One helpful, anonymous commentator pointed out that money needs to be easily *movable* and *transferable* and that it has to be *nonperishable*. With the qualifications like the Sparta example, I agree with these points, so let us add them collectively as another condition.

10   *Only animals with human or humanlike cognitive capacities can have money.* Dogs, for example, are very intelligent social animals, but if I leave a pile of dollar bills next to my dog's bed and train him to bring me a dollar bill every time he wants to be fed, even if I feed him only on receipt of the dollar bill, all the same, he is not buying anything with the money and it is not even money to him. Why not?

2. Social ontology

I think one of the reasons that the accounts of money I have seen are so inadequate is that they do not rest on an adequate account of social ontology in general. So, before I get into the special problems about money, I want to say something about social ontology.

We need a distinction between the epistemic sense of the objective-subjective distinction and an ontological sense of the distinction. So, for example, in the epistemic sense I can say that Barack Obama was president of the United States in 2015 – that is epistemically objective because it can be established as a matter of fact – but I can also say that Obama was a better president than George W. Bush – that is a matter of subjective opinion. Epistemic objectivity and subjectivity are always features of claims, statements, assertions, etc. Underlying that epistemic distinction is a distinction in modes of existence. Pains, tickles, and itches, as well as beliefs, hopes, and desires, have a mode of existence that depends on being experienced by a subject. They are ontologically subjective, whereas mountains and tectonic plates, electric charges, and avalanches exist no matter what anyone thinks. They are ontologically objective.

Related to that is another crucial distinction between those features of reality which are observer-relative, which depend for their very existence on being observed, thought about, attended to, or regarded in a certain way, and those that are independent of anybody's attitude or observation. Money, government, property, and marriage are all observer-relative phenomena, whereas such brute physical entities, such as mountains and planets, are observer-independent. Part of the interest of this distinction is that many phenomena, and it will turn out that money is one of them, which have a mode of existence that is observer-relative and therefore ontologically subjective, nonetheless admit of characterizations that are epistemically objective. It is, for example, an epistemically objective fact that I have a $20 bill in my hand even though the existence of $20 bills is observer-relative and thus contains elements of ontological subjectivity. It is an important point that the ontological subjectivity of a domain does not by itself imply that characterizations of phenomena in the domain must be epistemically subjective. All of this is going to be important when we get to money.

All functions are observer-relative. In general, we can say that function is a cause that serves a purpose and the purpose has to come from some intentionality, human or animal. Many species of animals can assign functions to objects. Think of birds' nests or the use of a stick by a chimpanzee to dig out ants for food. Human beings have a special capacity which, as far as I know, is unknown in other animal species, which is that they can impose functions on objects and other people where the function is not performed in virtue of the physical features of the person or object, or at least not the physical features alone, but it is performed in virtue of the fact that a certain *status* has been assigned to the person or object, and with that status there is a *function* that can be performed only in virtue of the *collective acceptance or recognition* of that status in the community in question. So the fact that Donald Trump is now president gives him a status, and with that status a certain set of powers, but these status functions, as I call them, can be performed only in virtue of their collective acceptance in the community in question.

Status functions are the key to understanding human civilization because they provide reasons for action that are independent of inclinations and desires. They provide deontic powers, which are rights, duties, obligations, permissions, and authorizations, etc., and those provide reasons for action which are independent of the other inclinations and desires of the agent in question. We live in a sea of status functions: marriage, universities, private property, nation-states, summer vacations, restaurants, organized religions, and cocktail parties are all status functions.

Among the status functions assigned by Status Function Declarations are certifications. I am physically able to drive a car no matter what anybody thinks, but to drive a car legally I have to be certified as a licensed driver. Such certifications are very common. For example, in the building where I have my office, the elevators are periodically inspected and certified as safe. Certification will be important when we consider certain kinds of money. Often, status functions are accompanied by *status indicators*, epistemic devices that enable anyone to perceive that the person or object has the status function. Driver's licenses, wedding rings, and police officers' uniforms are all examples.

With the exception of the values attaching intrinsically to certain mental phenomena, all values are observer-relative. Therefore, gold is valuable only relative to our attitudes. Value is not intrinsic to gold, nor to any other external object. The exceptional cases are those human mental states that have values intrinsically built into them. So, for example, a true belief is better than a false belief because it is part of the definition, part of what it is to be a belief that the belief succeeds if it is true and fails if it is false. Leaving out the intrinsic values of certain human mental phenomena, we can say that all values are observer-relative because value has to be assigned by some conscious agent, human or animal. And because values are assigned, they are observer-relative.

3. Status functions are created by Declaration

If, as I have said, status functions are the key to understanding human civilization, then how exactly are they created? It turns out they are all created by a certain type of speech act that I call a Declaration, where you make something the case by declaring it to be the case. J. L. Austin's performatives are good examples. When the chairman says, "The meeting is adjourned", he makes it the case that the meeting is adjourned by Declaration. The Status Function Declaration creates a status function by declaring it to exist. When it says on US currency, "This note is legal tender for all debts public and private", that utterance makes it the case by Declaration that the note is legal tender. The fact is not discovered by empirical investigation; it is created by Declaration. The bill is *declared* to be legal tender. Often the Status Function Declaration can be inexplicit. For example, two people can become involved in a love affair without anybody declaring, "This is a love affair".

It turns out that there is a class of status functions that differs strikingly from other status functions, and those are linguistic acts that create deontic powers. But we cannot say that the speech act status functions are created, like other status functions, by speech acts, or we would get an infinite regress. The infinite regress results from the following: If it turns out that all status functions are created by speech acts, then the status function which is the speech act must in turn be created by some further speech act, and so on infinitely.

To summarize, there are non-linguistic status functions which include private property, government, marriage, universities, cocktail parties, and summer vacations. All of those are created by a certain type of speech act, sometimes inexplicit, the Status Function Declaration. There are linguistic status functions which are speech acts, such as promises or statements. Speech act status functions are not typically created by external Declarations. If I say, "I promise to come and see you on Wednesday", that utterance creates a linguistic status function, a promise. But the speech act itself is not created by a further speech act, and the powers of the speech act do not exceed the semantic powers of the sentence. However, if the chairman says, "The meeting is adjourned", he creates a non-linguistic status function, the adjournment of the meeting. Here, the powers are created by the semantics, but the powers go beyond semantic powers.

4. Money is always a status function

What fact about this $20 bill makes it money? Well, this is not just money, but it is a paradigm case of a status function. The status function is a function that is performed not in virtue of the physical features of the object or person in question that has the status function, but in virtue of the fact that there is a collective acceptance that the object or person has a certain status and a function that can be performed only in virtue of the collective acceptance of that status. The $20 bill fits this definition perfectly because it does have a definite status of being a $20 bill in the United States. It performs the function in virtue of the collective recognition of that status. But the function is not performed in virtue of the physical structure. The physical structure is rather trivial. I emphasize these points because some people whose opinions I respect have said that the $20 bill is not money. According to Tony Lawson,[2] it is in fact an IOU, a promise to pay. But the problem with that is, if it is an IOU, I will presumably want to cash it and get paid in real money. But if I take it to the Treasury and ask that they redeem it, what they would in fact give me is another $20 bill (that is, if they did not think I was totally crazy).

In the first drafts of this text, I thought certain kinds of commodity money were not status functions. For example, at a time when gold and silver were commonly used as money, the value of the coin was supposedly exactly equal to the value of the gold or silver in the coin. This seems to be a case where the object performs its function solely in virtue of its physical structure. Of course the attachment of value is observer-relative and thus contains an element of ontological subjectivity – it is only because of our attitudes that gold and silver are valuable. They have no "intrinsic" value. But as long as the gold or silver is assigned a status solely in virtue of its physical structure, its structure as gold or as silver, then it seems it is not yet a status function.

This view now seems to me a mistake. What is the difference between exchanging lumps of gold for goods and services and having gold coins as money? There are several differences, at least these: the coinage typically involves a certification that there is so much gold in the coin. So the coin has a *certification status function*, because the government stamp guaranteed that it contained such and such amount of gold. Notice that the gold is measured in money, not the money in gold. We say, "This is a $20 gold piece", not "This amount of money is half an ounce". Furthermore, the use as money gives it a status function as "legal tender". If you owed somebody $20, a $20 gold piece constitutes payment, whereas an equivalent-sized lump of gold may not be accepted as such. Therefore, commodity money, if it is really money, is always a matter of status functions because deontic powers accrue to the money in virtue of the collective acceptance of their status as money. All money, to function as money, requires collective acceptance or recognition of its status as money, and for that reason, *all money is a status function*.

I said earlier that we need a distinction between *commodity* money, where commodities such as gold and silver are used as money; *contract* money, where a contract to pay the bearer is used as money; and *fiat* money. I abandon the terminology of *fiat* and replace it with *baseless* money, for two

---

2 See Tony Lawson, "Social Positioning and the Nature of Money", in *Cambridge Journal of Economics*, Vol. 40, No. 4, 2016, pp. 961–996.

reasons. First, all money is fiat money because it is created by a Status Function Declaration. Second, because the distinguishing feature of this third type is that it is not backed by anything. It is baseless. We can consider two such cases: the $20 bill is a case of baseless money, and the gold coin is a case of commodity money. What about the intermediate case, the case of contract money? Well, in the imagined evolution of money that I described above, it was impractical for people to carry gold and silver around with them, so they left it with the bank, and the banker issued certificates that were redeemable in gold and silver. The certificates were a promise to pay, hence a contract, and the contract money said that the bank would pay the bearer on demand so much in gold or silver. Contracts are status functions, but they are purely linguistic; they are promises. They are standing speech acts, and the standing speech act, the promise to pay in gold or silver, can function as money because the contract actually is exchangeable for the commodity. Contract money is valuable because, in theory at least, you can exchange the contract for some valuable commodity. Some genius discovered that they could issue more contracts than they actually have in gold or silver in the bank. If everybody rushes to the bank at once, the bank will fail, and such cases have happened many times throughout history. The fact that more contracts are issued than can possibly be fulfilled all at once, and that there is nothing in the contract to block simultaneous demands for fulfillment of all of them, is a *second example of the systematic deception involved in money*. The bearer of the contract thinks that his contract is fulfillable if the conditions stated in the contract are satisfied. But that is not really true, because if everybody wants his or her contract fulfilled at once, the bank or other agency will go bankrupt. How can money-issuing institutions get away with this? It is as if the city sold the right to sit in a seat on park benches and then sold more rights than there are seats on the benches. It is a systematic deception that more contracts are issued than can be redeemed. This is the second of several types of deception we will find in money.

To summarize our results so far, we found that there are three kinds of money. The first kind, commodity money, is a status function precisely to the extent that it is collectively recognized as money and not just as a commodity. Second, the case of contract money is a case where the semantics of the speech act are sufficient to guarantee the deontic powers. When money was freely exchangeable for gold, it said on the bill that the US Treasury agrees to pay the bearer $20 in gold on demand, and that is an actual promise. Because the speech act is an official speech act of the government, it is a status function in virtue of its semantics. Third, the purest case of the status functions of money is baseless money, where something becomes money in virtue of the imposition of a status function. The point is this: *all money is the result of the imposition of status functions by "fiat", and sometimes that imposition is in virtue of some other feature that the money-stuff has. These are the cases of commodity and contract money.* But even in these cases a lot of the money in the system will be baseless money because there will be more contracts issued than there is gold to back them and there will be more money in the economy than there is gold in the central bank and in circulation.

So far we have found two types of systematic deception involved in money. The first is where baseless money is disguised as contract money. It typically says on the bill that the Treasury will pay the bearer on demand so much money. It used to say this on US Federal Reserve notes, and as far as I know, it still says it on British currency. This is a deception because it implies that there is something distinct from the bill in virtue of which it has its value, and that the bill is redeemable in this further valuable entity. But there is no such entity. The most you could get would be another such bill. I assume this has to be a survivor of the actual practice in contract money of stating that the bill was a contract redeemable for gold or some other such commodity. But in the case of baseless money, there is no such "backing". There is just the bill itself. The second is the case of contract money, where more contracts are issued than there are quantities held by the contract issuer sufficient to redeem all of the contracts simultaneously.

The upshot of this discussion is that money is like various other types of status function in that something is money only if everybody believes that it is money and that everybody believes that everybody else believes that it is money and everybody believes that everybody else believes that everybody else believes that it is money and so on. Some money is believed to be money in virtue of some other feature. It is a valuable commodity or a contract to exchange the money for a valuable commodity, but these are in no way essential to its being money, and indeed, we will see that even these cases are misleading and involve certain kinds of deception.

5. Further forms of deception and money

It is of the essence of money, as I have described it, that it involves forms of deception. I do not say "lying" because that implies a conscious intentional liar. Also, the deception is not that of supposing it has intrinsic value. Outside of certain conscious states, nothing has intrinsic value. As far as intrinsic value is concerned, the special thing about money is that the value is at one remove. It has observer-relative value because it can be used to get many other things that have observer-relative value.

The first form of deception occurs where fiat money is disguised as contract money. It says on the £10 note that the bearer will be paid £10, thus giving the impression that the note derives its value like other forms of contract money from the things it can be redeemed for, which are quite distinct from the contract itself. However, to repeat, there is no such other thing. The "contract" is all there is to the money.

The second form of deception occurs when in the case of contract money more contract promises are made than can be simultaneously fulfilled.

A third form of deception occurs when banks create money by lending more money than they have. When the bank lends you $1,000, it need not have the $1,000. It creates money, literally, by setting up accounts for more money than it has. The only constraint on this deception is that the government sets reserve ratios where a certain percentage of the loan must be possessed by the bank. If the reserve ratio is 20%, then when the bank loans you the $1,000, they have to actually have $200 in the bank. The other $800 is pure creation because money, in the form of spendable bank deposits, now exists which did not previously exist.

The fourth, and most interesting, form of deception has to do with ontology. To understand this, go back to the Confederate $100 bill. Unlike the American $20 bill, it does not say that it is worth the value on its face. Rather, it says that two years after the cessation of hostilities between the Confederate States of America and the United States of America, the Confederate States will pay the bearer $100. But what exactly is a dollar such that the Confederacy will give the bearer 100 of them? Of course the Confederacy lost, but suppose they had won. What would they have given? What did they promise to give?

Basic to our conception of how we relate to reality is that most of reality consists of objects (things, entities, etc.). Look around and you will find yourself surrounded by objects – people, furniture, cars, houses, trees, not to mention planets, galaxies, blades of grass, and oceans. Objects have remarkable features. You can distinguish one from another, even those of the same type. This is one car, these are two cars. This is what enables us to count objects. Perhaps above all, objects are countable. Furthermore, you can re-identify the same object on different occasions, even though there have been changes in the object. This is still my car, the same one I had last year. These two features, countability and re-identifiability, have traditional names; they are called individuation and identity. Identity presupposes individuation. In order to say that it is *the same* car (identity), you have to be able to say that it is *a* car (individuation).

The ontological deception in money can be stated quite simply. The vocabulary contains the implication of individuation and identity, but money does not satisfy these conditions. We can say, "I borrowed $20 from you and I am paying back the $20", and that looks a lot like saying, "I borrowed your car and I am giving back the car". But though these sentences look alike, their logical structure is, in fact, quite different. In order to give back your car, I have to give back the same material object that I borrowed. But in order to return your $20, any number of physical objects will suffice. Indeed, no physical object at all is necessary. This is because, in order to function as money, money does not require any physical existence at all, but only representations that record the amount of money that agents have and the amount that they are transferring in economic transactions.

To get at these issues, we have to ask, what is it that I have exactly when I have money in my bank account, granted that I need not have any physical object whatever? There are representations of the amount of money I have, and what exactly do those representations represent? They do not represent any physical object whatsoever. They represent power, the specific power to buy. *In addition to such powers, there is no such thing as money.* We can embody those powers in coins and bills. The coins and bills are literally money and not *representations* of anything, but in order for there to be the function of money, there need not be coins, bills or any physical realization whatsoever. All there needs to be are well-defined representations of amounts of money such that you can buy something by transferring the amount in your representation to somebody else's representation.

What do you have 100 of when you have $100? Strictly speaking, you do not have 100 of anything. What you have is a certain power, and that power is measured roughly by assigning a numerical value. This is why no physical object is necessary to have money. All you need is some way of representing how much money you have. And this is why we get the illusion that money has absolute digital value, because it can always be measured on a digital scale. Leaving out taxes and other debts, if all the prices double tonight, you have lost half your money because you have lost half of your power even though the digital sum you have remained exactly the same.

The deception inherent in money comes out in the following. The requirement that money be digital implies that any storage of money we have is numerically specifiable. However, because the essence of money is deontic power, that specification does not specify the specific amount of power that the possessor of the money has. The power is only relative to the prices of the goods and services that the possessor might want to buy, and debts, such as taxes for example, can be imposed on the possessor. The power in money is never absolute but only relative to the price, including tax, structures. This is disguised from us by the fact that we think we have such and such amount of money.

This deception can manifest in countless ways. For example, public authorities recognize that people would much rather have the price of goods and services rise than a reduction in their salaries. The effects are exactly the same. Business people are shrewd enough to see that a tax break is just as good as a rise in income because it is, in effect, a rise in income. In the salary case, people think they are actually getting a fixed amount of money in their salary. But the essence of money is power, and the power is not fixed by the numerical value but only the numerical value relative to prices and debts.

Governments, encouraged by their economists, tend to like a small, continuous rate of inflation. This is because the public has the illusion that they have more money when their salaries are increased to match the inflation, whereas in fact they may be suffering a decline in their standard of living, and they almost certainly are in the United States because tax rates are increasing as they move into higher tax brackets.

In my lifetime, the Carter administration was one of the worst offenders regarding inflation. In some years, there was a 15% rate of inflation when I was receiving a 5% annual increase in my salary. Carter and his economists did not think this was a problem. Many people, including me, did, and this was one of the reasons he was defeated after one term. Money consists entirely in power, specifically deontic power to buy, pay, and close debts. Ontologically speaking, there is nothing else.

The system only works on two conditions. First, it must be countable: you must be able to count how much money you have, how much money you have paid, how much money you owe, etc. And second, there must be a system of representation, so at any given moment there is an accurate representation of these values. These two features, countability and representation, inevitably give rise to the deception. We think there must be some entities (things, objects) which we are counting and representing.

6. Money and deception, a summary

To summarize, there are several forms of systematic deception that are endemic to money.

First, a deception occurs when baseless money is disguised as contract money in the way that I described. It says on the baseless money that it is contract to "pay the bearer on demand" in money. But there is no such thing as money other than the sort of money it is.

Second, a deception occurs when government, bank, or other agents issue more contracts to pay than they can simultaneously satisfy. If I hold in my hand a contract to pay me, the bearer, on demand three ounces of gold, I reasonably assume that the satisfaction of my demand is not dependent on the behavior of other contract holders. Unless the contract states otherwise, I assume it can be satisfied anytime. But that is a deception. The contract can be fulfilled only on the condition that other contract holders do not insist their contracts be satisfied. If a sufficient number simultaneously insist on satisfaction, the bank will run out of resources and will be forced to default.

That is, it will be unable to meet its contractual obligations and, in many cases, will be forced to close, to declare bankruptcy.

Third, when the bank lends you money, you think this is just like borrowing money on interest from a friend or relative. But friends and relatives cannot lend you money they do not have. The bank precisely lends you money it does not have, and thus it literally creates money.

Fourth, another deception occurs when I am the possessor of, let us say, $100 (or pounds, euros, etc.). I naturally assume there is a class of such entities and that I possess 100 of them. But there are no such entities. Even if I have 100 $1 bills, the actual bills function only as *forms of power* and the amount of power is not fixed by the numerical values. It is fixed by the relation of the number I have to the prices of goods, services, and debts. If the prices double, my power is cut in half even though my number of 100 remains constant.

It is a mistake to think that the 100 $1 bills are representations, because they do not represent anything. If I have $100 in my bank account, there is indeed in the bank a representation of how much money I have in the account. But the actual bills in my hand do not in that way represent anything. They actually are powers and nothing more because, as their possessor, I have the power to buy things and pay debts with them.

Fifth, the final deception I have not so far discussed, but I think is implicit in pretty much everything I have said, is that we have the illusion, and this illusion is fostered in all sorts of different ways, that the money in our hand is only money because it is *backed by* something. It may be backed by gold, promises, debts, or by the US government, but it has to be backed by something. This is a falsehood, and I hope that it is obvious. Even in the cases where there is the appearance of being backed by something, commodity money and contract money, much of the stuff that passes for money has no backing. Even under the gold standard, the amount of gold in circulation or in the bank is unlikely to be as great as all the money in the economy.

7. What is money?

I began this chapter by saying that I had in my hand a US $20 bill. I believe we now have enough tools to be able to analyze that statement. What facts make it the case that the United States has the institution of money, and what fact about me makes it the case that I have such and such an amount of money? Any such analysis will give us an analysis of money. Because we are not concerned with the money of a specific country, and because, as we have seen, money need not take the form of currency, the statement we need to analyze is much more general. We assume that there is a community C, and that it contains agents A1, A2, A3, etc. We assume that this community has certain general practices, recognized by and engaged in by the agents of

C. We assume that they assign numerical values of (what we will call) Units of something to the members. Intuitively, we think these Units are dollars, pounds, etc., but we do not use these concepts and just say that, at any point in time, any A of C will have a certain number of N Units, where N may be equal to zero if A is broke. In earlier drafts, I counted people who are in debt as having negative Units. But that does not really seem to work very well,[3] so I am now counting zero Units as the limiting case. What we are trying to analyze is, what fact about those Units makes them money. There are two aspects to the analysis: First, what is it for a community C to have the institution of money? Second, what is it for an individual A with that community to have a specific amount of money? No individual can have money unless there is a collective practice of money within his or her community.

But our analysis must make no reference explicitly or implicitly to money. Therefore, we cannot mention buying, selling, etc. The analysis must be given entirely in nonmonetary concepts. Since we are trying to analyze money in terms of its deontology, we can use the deontic concepts because they are quite general and have no special reference to money. The analysis makes explicit what is meant by saying money is essentially social. We assume that the society has recognized Units, which we intuitively think of as dollars, pounds, euros, etc., but we cannot use such concepts. Our task is to explain what facts about dollars, etc., makes them money. Here are the statements we need to analyze.

A community C has money measured in Units. A person or subject S in a community C has money to the amount of N Units.

I will give the analysis as a set of numbered propositions, followed by an attempt to explain it in parentheses. The parentheses are not part of the analysis.

Here is the analysis:

1   The community C has the practice of assigning numerical values N of Units to agents A1, A2, A3, etc., in C. Each A in C is the owner of N Units, where the limiting case is $N = 0$. To put this in a way that makes the quantifier scope explicit, we can say:

> At any time T, and for any A in C, there is some N such that A has N Units at T. (This just says that, at any time, everybody has a certain amount of money [including no money at all as a limiting case].) The assignments of Units may be for all sorts of reasons: e.g. payments, inheritance, theft, pensions, finding money in the streets,

---

3 Why not? Major debts such as mortgages are typically incurred to buy valuable property which increases in value. Holders of such debts have an increased net worth in dollars as a result of the debt. To explain this requires an analysis of liquidity, and that is beyond the scope of this chapter.

winning bets, etc. The agents may be people, families, corporations, gangs, etc. The point is, at any given moment each agent has a certain amount of money, including zero amount for people who are broke. However, the Units, so far, are not necessarily money. So far, they could be cans of beer or pairs of pants. What do they have to have to be money?

2   The Units are believed to be valuable by all the members of C, but they are believed to be valuable only because each member believes that all the others believe that they are valuable. Each member believes that all the other members believe that each member believes that all the other members believe that the Units are valuable, and so on up in a potentially infinite fashion.

> (These potentially infinite but benign regresses in collective intentionality are familiar in analyses of collective intentionality. I have tried to frame it in ways that avoid traditional controversies about whether collective intentionality of the form "we intend", "we believe", etc., can be analyzed as individual intentionality, "I intend", "I believe", etc.)

3   The Units are believed to be valuable, not for their own sake, but because each Agent possessing Units has certain powers as a result of that possession.

> (The analysis of these powers explains what makes the Units money.)

4   C has the practice whereby Units can be transferred from one Agent to another.

> (This may be by buying and selling, but also by taxation, extortion, gifts, etc. The point is, if you cannot transfer it from one agent to another, it is not money. Money is not just social, but it is socially transferable.)

5   The possessor A of N Units can exchange those units either all or in part for goods and services possessed by other Agents. Typically, both parties will make the exchange voluntarily, but it can also be forced, as when the government forces people to buy health insurance. The exchange results in the new possessor ("the buyer") acquiring deontic powers over the goods and services, the objects of the exchange, and the agent surrendering the goods and services ("the seller") acquiring deontic powers over the N Units exchanged.

> (This is the ability to buy and sell.)

6   To the extent that any Agent is under obligations specified in Units, the obligations may be removed by giving to the holder of the obligation the number of Units in question.

      (This is the ability to pay debts.)

This, then, is the analysis of money. Can it really be this simple? Perhaps it is. Money, so analyzed, is essentially collective, and the collective practice assigns deontic powers to the individual agent, where the agents need not be human individuals but corporations, etc. Essentially, the two abilities are the ability to buy and sell and the ability to incur and pay debts. What about our features, such as money as a store of value and measure of value? I think they follow from the analysis as stated. If you have Units that function the way I have described, you can always state, "I have so many Units in my bank account, under the mattress, etc." I can also ask of any exchangeable object, "How many Units is it worth?"

I believe that this explains all of the conditions that we stated for something to be money, with the exception of why animals cannot do it. The reason why my dog, Tarski, cannot operate with money, cannot possess money, spend money, etc., is that in order to do that, you have to be able to operate with a lot of rather complex deontic concepts. In particular, you have to be able to operate with the deontic concepts of rights, duties, and obligations. You have to see that possessing money gives you deontic powers and that those who owe you money have deontic obligations. In order to have those thoughts, you have to have a language. Thus, the short answer to why animals cannot do it is, in order to do it, you have to have something like a human language. A bee language or animal signaling system is not enough. You have to be able to think with a much richer set of categories, and that requires something like a human language.

2 The color of money

Maurizio Ferraris[1]

0. Introduction: which came first, the chicken or the egg?

Which came first, money or the value we attribute to it? This question recalls another one, asked by Plato: are things pious because God loves them or does God love them because they are pious? The answer at first seems easy: value (or at least need) precedes money. But maybe it is not so. Of course, when we handle money we have the impression that it has value because the community in which we live feels that it does. But it is difficult to ignore the fact that when I handle money, I have the impression that the value lies in the money, not in my head: I may have wrong theories on money, or no theory at all, without compromising the value of the note I am holding. This is a psychological and philosophical enigma to solve: if money had value because we thought it did, why is it not enough to change our mind for it to lose value? And if we are not the ones who give money its value, then who is?

This question is similar to the chicken and egg problem. So, to avoid the circularity and solve the dilemma, I propose to distinguish two levels: a manifest level, reflecting our immediate intuition, where value precedes money; and a deep level, which is much less intuitive, where money determines value instead. I will try to show the legitimacy of the latter. So, after presenting the manifest image, I will look into the deep structure by which money (a paradigmatic document) precedes and produces its value. This fact is manifested in the sacred respect that "the color of money" (to quote an old movie) arouses in its worshippers – namely, us all – no matter the ethical convictions, psychological dispositions, ideological orientations that

---

1 As aforementioned, the first version of this chapter was originally published in Italian in the book *Il denaro e i suoi inganni* (by John Rogers Searle and Maurizio Ferraris, edited and with an essay by Angela Condello, Einaudi, 2018).

guide us in earning it or not, wanting it or not, investing it rationally or wasting it all, saving it or throwing it out the window.

First I will deal with epistemology, that is, what we know (or believe we know) of social reality. In other words, I will deal with the egg, distinguishing between the manifest image (the idea that social reality is constructed by intentionality, our thoughts and representations) and the deep structure (the idea that social reality emerges from what I call "documentality": a system of recordings with recognizable forms that is the origin of social objects, including money). Then I will move on to ontology, that is, the processes underlying the formation of the value and normativity of money and, more generally, of documentality. In other words, I will deal with the chicken, trying to account for the deep structure by answering the question: what allows for documentality (social objects), if intentionality as a living act is not the ultimate foundation of social reality? Finally, I will introduce a third dimension that, in my opinion, is necessary to explain the nature of money and of social reality in general: namely, technology. By this term I mean the actions we perform in the social world, which most of the time are not guided by clear knowledge of that world, and therefore appear as competence without understanding.

The underlying idea is that – contrary to what the social contract theorists believe – we come into contact with the ontological dimension, in this case with the social forces (obligation, responsibility, motivation, intentionality), not through understanding (epistemology) but through action. When I handle money, I do not apply an economic theory (or at least a real economic theory: maybe I think money has value because it can be traded with gold, and of course I do not wonder why gold has value); I simply act. This attitude is the fundamental character of my relationship with reality in general. Little by little, through action, I can, though not necessarily have to, become aware of what I do, so that competence becomes understanding: that is, (here is the thesis I would like to conclude) ontology turns into epistemology.

To get an idea of my perspective, imagine three concentric spheres (see Figure 2.1).

The first is epistemology, which is very small, because the sphere of what we know is not very big. The second and intermediate one is that of technology: what we do, which is far more than what we know. The third, finally, is that of ontology, the vast sphere of what there is in the social world and, even more so, in the natural world. Indeed, I am convinced that the enigma of money – like the many enigmas it carries with it – can only be solved by keeping in mind all three dimensions. This is why I have dared to take up more space than Searle in my contribution – which in a way is also a tribute to the memorable discussion between him and Jacques Derrida that happened

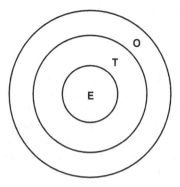

Figure 2.1 The relationship between Epistemology, Ontology, and Technology

almost half a century ago, where the page ratio of the essays in question was roughly of 1 to 10.[2] But fortunately time leads to understanding, and the epic disagreement between Searle and Derrida here gives way, I hope, to a fundamental agreement between Searle and myself, or at least to the possible integration of our views.

1. Epistemology

The epistemological form of society is not transparent to its members more than consciousness is transparent to the subjects. The fact that those things are the closest to us is anything but an advantage: it is rather a case of thing being "a little too obvious" things, like the purloined letter of Poe's novel, which for that very reason escape our observation and our conscience. That is why to answer the question of what gives value to a piece of paper one cannot point to some evidence, but rather has to solve a riddle – or at least try to do so. One needs to lift a veil that makes mysterious not only the nature of money, but the whole sphere of social normativity: What is the secular sacrament that transforms a human being into a doctor (authorized to cure), a license holder (authorized to drive), a recipient of a call-up paper or a payment order (required to show up in the barracks or to pay)? After all, that of the purloined letter is not a simple literary suggestion: because in all these cases there is a piece of paper involved – although, of course, the paper might be replaced with plastic, metal (still in use for money),

2 For some of the essays in question, see Jacques Derrida, *Limited Inc.*, Northwestern University Press, Evanston, IL, 1988.

tattoos, gallons, distinctive signs of all sorts and quite picturesque, or simply recordings on a computer or a mobile phone.

1.1. Analysis

To solve a riddle, one must first of all understand the terms involved. In this first section I will therefore adopt a style closer to Searle's, and I will try to resolve the alternative between intentionality and documentality. I will conceive the former as the manifest image (the way in which social reality appears to us, in whose framework we interpret money) and the latter as the deep structure (the fundamental core of social reality, which naturally escapes our immediate intuition).

1.2. Manifest image

"Manifest image" does not mean "false image". Seeing society and its objects, including money, as the outcome of our intentionality (money has value because we think it does, laws apply because we think they do) is actually the way most adults in our age relate to the social world. So, the most direct and intuitive way to explain the functioning of money and social reality as a whole is intentionalism, whose most illustrious interpreter is indeed John Searle.[3] For intentionalists, the constitutive rule of objects is X counts as Y in C: X (the physical object, e.g. a piece of paper) counts as Y (social object, e.g. a banknote) in context C, because of collective intentionality.

The intentionalist perspective has a twofold structure. Its first element is the claim that social reality is constructed by us. In fact, when we reflect on our relationship with money, titles, works of art, we have the idea that these objects are socially what they are because we collectively decide that they are money, titles, works of art. The second element is the thesis that this "us" manifests itself as collective intentionality (a close relative of Rousseau's general will, of Montesquieu's spirit of the laws, and after all of the spirit in the Christian and Hegelian sense). Once again, the manifest image meets our fundamental intuitions. In fact, when we pay, we have the impression that both us and the recipient of money share the conviction that money has value because we believe so.

---

3 John R. Searle, *The Construction of Social Reality*, The Free Press, New York, 1995 and id., *Making the Social World: The Structure of Human Civilization*, Oxford University Press, Oxford, 2010; see also John Langshaw Austin, *How to Do Things With Words*, Harvard University Press, Cambridge, MA, 1962.

However, the manifest image leaves a few things unexplained. First of all, it is unclear what is meant by "collective intentionality": a vague notion that seems to not only cover obvious sharing phenomena ("Should we take a walk?", "Let's have a coffee") but also chimerical constructs like the general will. It is also unclear what its spatial-temporal location would be, provided there is one. Instead, it is very clear what individual intentionality may be – something that can be shared and coordinated with other ones based on a document. All in all, collective intentionality is but a legal fiction comparable to the generalizability test of the Kantian moral imperative: when the court issues a ruling "in the name of the Italian people" it is acting as the representative of a collective intentionality? Of course not: it simply means that the decision is not arbitrary, and is taken in compliance with the law. Likewise, expressions such as "the Court ruled" do not show collective intentionality, but simply a decision (taken by majority or unanimously), that is, the numerical predominance of individual intentions.

Secondly, the intentionalist perspective does not account for negative entities, such as debts – it is difficult to find a physical X corresponding to the negative social Y.[4] The same difficulty applies to electronic money. If I pay with my cell phone, is the physical X the phone? If it is so then the same object has two prices: a sales price and a variable price, which manifests itself through its purchasing potential, which could hardly be considered a property of the phone as a physical X. Finally, collective intentionality interprets society in terms of harmony and consensus rather than in terms of conflict, disagreement, contradiction: and yet the latter is the way in which social reality has always appeared to us, from the *Iliad* to today. Society, as well as normativity (laws, obligations, institutions, rules, prohibitions), does not manifest itself in consensus but in conflict. Indeed, norms are mainly perceived when they are in conflict with our instincts and our immediate dispositions, clashing with what we would like to do. And collective intentionality only explains some situations in which normativity is weak: a walk or a picnic, not a board of directors, a major state, or a court. The same sharing of collective intentions that seems to unite the members of a football team or the musicians of an orchestra is the result of a document-based normativity: in the first case the coach presenting the game schemes and the constraints imposed by the rules of football, in the second the director (whose presence would be completely useless, like that of coaches and generals, if there really was collective intentionality) and the sheet music.

4 John R. Searle and Barry Smith, "The Construction of Social Reality: An Exchange", in *American Journal of Economics and Sociology*, Vol. LXII, No. 1, January 2003, pp. 285–309.

It is not surprising that the manifest image faces the same difficulties as the social contract in politics, and as dualism in the theory of the mind. These difficulties become particularly notable in the case of money, whose structure would be divided into a spiritual part that is in us (the value attributed to money), and into a material and accidental part, perhaps invented by Theuth or Cadmus. Intentionality would be acting as a collective pineal gland, called to link the *res cogitans* (the value, the social object) with the *res extensa* (the piece of paper, the physical object). In short, the manifest image undoubtedly explains certain social acts – there is no question that a parliament constructs something when promulgating a law (even if it is worth noting that the form of the law and its context are already there, and therefore it isn't an absolute construction). However, the intentionalist explanation as such is no less mythological than an explanation of morality for which the ten commandments are actually the manifestation of God's will to Moses, or a stipulation between Moses and YHWH, or even a referendum held at the feet of Mount Sinai.

In fact, there are many empirical circumstances disproving the intentionalist explanation. In addition to the obvious difficulty that it is impossible to determine when and how the "invention" of money actually took place (and the term "invention", as we shall see, is as inappropriate here as when referred to the "invention" of fire), and in addition to the even greater difficulty of clarifying the nature of collective intentionality, which has the burden of proof, the intentionalist explanation makes money a fragile invention, which could be rejected at any time by the mere cessation of consensus. But it is not so. The reduction (not the disappearance) of monetization in the Middle Ages was not the result of consensual renunciation, but depended on the rarity of coins, which were no longer able to cover the amount of real exchanges, and the enemy's money is still valid in times of war (as Wittgenstein's father well knew, investing his capital on the titles of the Entente).

Also, whatever collective intentionality wants, or does not want – and provided such a unitary feeling exists – when a state prints too many banknotes people do not become richer (as they should if the value of money depended on collective intentionality) but poorer, and money loses value. Indeed, although everyone agrees that DM1,000 is a lot of money, why is it that they can suddenly be worth nothing, and one has to switch to banknotes like 100,000, or 1,000,000? More than with a collective intentionality we would be dealing with a collectively masochistic intentionality. Lastly, if collective intentionality determined the value of money, it would be impossible to explain phenomena such as financial crises. Neither the latter nor natural phenomena can be controlled, but with a single and significant difference, which relates to the deep structure: namely that the disappearance of collective memory and documents would end – albeit dramatically, meaning the end of civilization – a financial crisis, but it would not be able to end rain, nor to question the gravitational law.

1.3. Deep structure

There are two main theses reflecting the deep structure. The first is that collective intentionality does not exist; instead, there is an often conflicting social interaction that is made possible by the use of documents (both in the strict and in the broad sense: institutions, rituals, transmitted behaviors) that coordinate individual actions and intentions. The second is that the color of money exerts its prestige on individual intentions without any intervention of collective intentionality – for the very good reason that a non-existent entity has no causal value – and based on the sole force of what I call "documentality".[5] By this term I do not mean the sphere of the intentions that exist in our mind, but that of social recordings, from the promise onward, which exist both out of our minds – in archives, wallets, cell phones – and in them, but as an external element: the memory of the word given, which is no longer entirely ours, unlike what happens to so many other thoughts that belong to us and only to us.

The crucial role of recording is very clear in the case of money. I have a note in my hand, and I can pay the bill at the restaurant. I can do so also with a debit card, with a cell phone, or photographing a barcode on the bill. What do these operations have in common? The fact that there are recordings – analogue or digital codes on my account, analogue or digital memories in my pockets – like paper tickets, plastic cards, or even a phone, which can do a lot of things because it has a lot of memory, which results in a great computational capacity. So, money is a form of recording; in fact all money can be traced back to this origin and function – and all that can accomplish this function can act as money. There is *no change* in terms of the nature of money occurring between a note, a card, and pure memory: what occurs is rather a revelation of what money really is, namely the recording of a numerical value that, through recording itself, acquires economic value.

If we understand that the essence of money is recording (according to the rule Object = Recorded Act, which is particularly clear with banknotes, where the act is a relation between the central bank and the anonymous

---

5 See Maurizio Ferraris, *Where Are You? An Ontology of the Cell Phone*, Fordham University Press, New York, NY, 2014; id., *Documentality: Why It Is Necessary to Leave Traces*, Fordham University Press, New York, 2012 and id., *Mobilitazione totale*, Laterza, Roma-Bari, 2014.

holder of the money), we can also understand why, before bank cards, people used coins (perhaps of gold, a material that does not rust), or shells, or salt sacks: all discrete portions that can be counted, generating an archive; that can be subdivided, facilitating payments; that can be kept in a limited space (for this reason only, by the way, coins are better than salt bags). The power behind the color of money, recording (that is, what is also the genetic principle of the form), is the principle underlying social normativity as a whole. According to what we have just said, documentality is the principle of responsibility, which in turn originates normativity – indeed, and more exactly, it is the mystical foundation of authority. In this sense, the essence of money is manifested in the bitcoin, and retrospectively the bitcoin realizes the value of the gold coin, of gold, and of salt. The digital currency, in fact, is nothing but the memory trace of the transaction, a pure document that has no external rooting, if not a secure and public record (the blockchain) that registers the transaction and acts as its guarantor.

This, like other empirical facts, proves the validity of documentalism. Society cannot do without inscriptions and recordings, archives and documents, and without the arche-technology of writing, which is the prototypical form of recording. Moreover, without recording there would not and could not be legal institutions, obligations, guarantees, and rights. So, justice would never have been fully realized, as it is intrinsically social. Documents do not only act as regulators in the economy and in the legal sphere, but are the producers of values, norms, cultures, conflicts, up to determining (through education and imitation) individual intentionality and allowing (through sharing) for collective intentionality. Despite appearances, it is the document that creates the value, not the value that produces the document: gold is not worth it because it is gold, but because it has characteristics (the same ones that make it a useful metal in jewelry) that make it a durable and malleable document medium.

1.4. Pentecost or emergence

The contraposition between intentionalism and documentalism implies a metaphysical problem. Considering (collective and individual) intentionality as a primitive means in fact embracing what I call "Pentecostal meaning": that is, postulating the existence of a meaning previous to and independent of the forms in which it is expressed and of the ways in which it is imprinted – that is, the psychological and social equivalent of Cartesian dualism. It means representing a pattern of this kind: in the mind there are meanings that are expressed through words, which in turn are represented in writing. So, meaning might exist even if unexpressed, and, most importantly, meaning has no genesis: it has always existed or has fallen from the sky.[6] This model is found in most theories of humankind and of society. In the theory of humankind it is postulated that there is an in-itself, human nature, which is alienated by external conditions, usually associated with technology, and which must be restored through a return to human nature as it really and naturally (i.e. ideally or fantastically) is. In the theory of society, the origin of the social world is placed precisely in collective intentionality, which manifests itself through a contract from which society originates.

Indeed, from the intentionalist perspective, money and its normative power are a variation of the social contract: it is agreed to give value to a piece of paper, or gold, a shell, or a bag of salt, just as it is agreed to regulate society in a certain way. The counterpart of this approach, in theory of the mind, is the postulate of a *res cogitans*, distinct and independent from the *res extensa*. All of this is based on a precise topology: meaning, spirit, idea, and conscience are inside; signifier, letter, expression, and action are outside. Conversely, the documentalist explanation calls for an emerging meaning (meaning comes from act and recording) instead of a Pentecostal one (meaning precedes act and recording). If Pentecostal meaning is conceived as independent and anterior to expression and recording, emergent meaning, on the contrary, recognizes its dependence on both,[7] and proposes a Copernican revolution that consists in overturning the traditional structure and conceiving intentionality (the spirit, the idea, the will, and the purpose) as successive and derivative, rather than as previous and foundational, compared to the forms of fixation (the letter, the expression, the norm). More radically, the deep structure argues that *documentality is a condition of intentionality.*

This change of perspective overcomes the difficulties raised by the manifest image, and in particular it answers the question why, if social reality is constructed, it is so difficult to change it. The answer is precisely that the manifest image hides an essential point: *the fact that social objects are constructed does not mean that social reality is constructed.* Like money, society is not constructed but emerges. Above all, society is not just a human

---

6 This expression has a very concrete reference: Giuseppe Sermonti (*L'alfabeto scende dalle stelle. Sull'origine della scrittura*, Mimesis, Milano-Udine, 2009) convincingly illustrates the astral origins of the alphabet, modeled upon star signs and the observation of the sky.

7 It is worth noting that re*cor*ding – registration and fixation into documents – etymologically refers to the heart (*cor*), just as the Italian verb ri*cor*dare, to *learn by heart, apprendre par coeur*. This shows the proximity between external and internal recording, as well as the fact that documentality underlies intentionality already at the level of conscience. The latter, moreover, is never an isolated conscience, a monad, but always something immersed in the world, subject to social interactions, and therefore with a much more fragile internal/external separation than suggested by the problematic difference between *res extensa* and *res cogitans*.

fact.[8] Society is not simply composed of humans, but includes dimensions other than human (animals, for example), or superhuman (myths, which are constitutive elements of the social world: transcendental structures that make us human and not tales invented by humans). If it is difficult to imagine non-human animals investing in the stock exchange (but not exchanging banknotes!), it is even more difficult to imagine that our forms of social organization (dominance structures, elementary relationships of kinship, taboos) have no relation of continuity with our animal past. Likewise, it is difficult to imagine a human social activity that is not decisively conditioned by its technical forms of realization, as well as by the natural environment in which it takes place (which is implicit, for example, in the notion of geopolitics).

So, money, very simply, is a document like any other: it's like a passport, for example, sharing its complicated decorations and characteristic colors (blue for Americans, red for Europeans, green for Arabs). With a passport a state authorizes a citizen to expatriate (so it was originally) and with a banknote it authorizes him to buy. Since the citizens who want to buy are far more numerous than those who want to expatriate, there are more banknotes than passports. And since money goes hand in hand, banknotes are not nominal, and – as exchanges are made quickly and possibly by illiterate people – to prevent misunderstandings in most countries (albeit with the significant exception of the United States) banknotes have different sizes and colors, so that money could be defined as the documents of those who cannot read. In addition, both with passports and with banknotes, the state does not invent anything new, but merely gives a paper form to ways of fixing acts and quantifying value that originated in our animal past and whose evolution coincides with the evolution of human cultures.

The enigma of money is thus solved. But there is an even more difficult puzzle still to be solved. Consider the strange authority that a piece of paper, or a recording on the phone, exerts on humans and their individual

---

8 For a critique of anthropocentric social ontology cf. Brian Epstein, *The Ant Trap: Rebuilding the Foundations of the Social Sciences*, Oxford University Press, Oxford, 2015. Yet, the intuition is ancient. Prodicus of Ceos (born between 470 and 460 BCE) argues that social reality and culture should not be studied as a world in its own right, but as an evolution of natural reality made possible by the emergence of technology, understood as the art of building tools that bring benefits to human beings within the natural world. From this perspective, Prodicus explains the birth of religion as a cult of natural goods and technical tools that make human existence easier. Gods, according to Prodicus, are nothing more than the mythization of these goods and instruments, or of the people who made them available: "things which nourish and benefit humans were first considered and honoured as gods, and later the discoverers of foods, shelters, and the other arts, such as Demeter, Dionysus, and the Dioscuri" (DK, 84 B 5). I thank Enrico Terrone for these precious considerations.

intentionality (whose existence, of course, I do not deny). Where does it come from? Karl Marx used to explain it through the tale of an intentionality that gives value to money and then forgets about it, now seeing value as something external and objective. However, Marx did not explain why, even after this revelation was made in Marxist texts, humankind carried on making the same mistake. Of course, the reason is that Marx's tale was indeed a tale, much like Feuerbach's myth by which humans first create gods and then end up believing in them. Let's be honest: people are stupid, but not that stupid. There has to be another explanation, which should not be sought in epistemology, in the shape the social world takes before us when we know it, but in ontology: the power (or better, powers) making up the essence of the world – in the case of money, of course, the social world.

2. Ontology

As I have said, epistemology is the form, that is, the structure of social objects and acts (which I described in the previous section). Ontology, on the other hand, is the power, that is, what mobilizes the social structures. It is no coincidence that they are traditionally interpreted in terms of social forces, class struggles, conflicts of interest, etc. – that is, in dynamic terms. (To understand this relationship in an intuitive way, imagine the relationship between ontology and epistemology as the one between will and representation in Schopenhauer, a terrible way to describe the natural world, but excellent for the social world.) What makes society social, in short, is power. Except that, as I will now argue, this power cannot take place in the absence of form, i.e. epistemology and documentality.

2.1. Dialectic

Here of course my argument will formally and substantially differ from Searle's. His social ontology, in fact, starts from the methodological choice not to thematize the two crucial poles of social ontology, which he places on the "background": that is, the whole of obvious beliefs we all share with regards to reality and collective intentionality. In a way, Searle chooses to treat them as noumena, things in themselves that are both really close and out of reach, while focusing on the intermediate structures of the manifest image. But as I have promised to talk about the deep structure I cannot use his same strategy and have to venture into the sphere of dialectic, the territory that the usually moderate Immanuel Kant defines in romantic, titanic, and sublime terms, with talk of mists and ice. In reality, this adventure is not as risky as Kant suggests, influenced by the reading of narratives of explorations and shipwrecks: it simply means going from the conditional to the condition. In a word, there is a social world that is so and so. What must be the ontological conditions that allow the social world to be what it is? The question may look risky, but – here's what I say to those who stick to the analysis – is it not even more risky to not want to know, perhaps ending up referring to problematic entities such as collective intentionality?

2.2. Necessary condition

The first stage of my dialectics deals with something obvious, and strictly speaking is still marked by an analytical attitude. The point is to demonstrate that, according to our ordinary experience, documentality is a necessary condition for social reality. Which is to say that without documentality (in the broad sense I have already specified) we would not have social reality. Indeed, this is an obvious consequence of the constitutive law Object = Recorded Act, which can be proved by simple counterfactuals: A stock exchange session without price lists, a marriage without registers, a sale without a contract, a trial without a sentence would all be nothing but frivolous exercises, and I doubt you would have bothered reading this book if you knew you'd forget everything you read. Therefore, documentality is what allows for social objects – things like promises, bets, assignments, and money, which require acts of communication, but must set themselves as recordings, otherwise they would remain empty words.

In addition to this consideration, which is indeed the mere analytical development of the constitutive law, there are elements which are not analytic. Documents, in fact, do not merely preserve social objects, but affect intentionality itself, confirming the dependence of ontology on epistemology that I have presented as a salient feature of the social world. The role of documentality in the constitution of intentionality – in the first, more obvious and elementary sense – concerns the benefits ensured by the sharing of plans in coordinated actions. The possibility of a joint action, which is undeniable but derived, lies in the production of documentality, from rock paintings to the complicated architecture of orders underlying a general mobilization. An action organized based on written documents is the secret of military effectiveness, but more extensively it is the foundation of social action, as evidenced by the importance of bureaucracy in the formation and management of power.

In this sense, documents are not just helpful tools, but are the basis of mass social action, and generate central phenomena of social reality such as authority, hierarchy, division of labor, responsibility, and punishment. Even concepts that apparently have nothing to do with documents, such as abuse of power, are explained precisely through the paradigm of documentality: abusing one's power means in fact failing to respect a mandate set by a contract, or by rites and customs, that is, it only takes place in a condition of high documentality.[9] It may be true that, as Napoleon maintained, battles are won by keeping the spirits up; but it remains to be explained why this spiritual state of mind collapses in the absence of orders, documents, instructions. Napoleon knew this better than anyone else, given that he was the first to demand a portable printing press in order to spread the orders on the battlefield in multiple copies.

This also holds in so-called societies without writing (I insist on this because the sphere of writing is hard to pinpoint precisely), where documentality manifests itself in myths and in the use of complicated rituals handed down over time. This is documentality and not intentionality because, in most cases, it consists of actions whose meaning is unknown to the social actors[10] and which take place, also topologically, outside of consciousness: in space and through movements. The actions and technology that underlie our everyday expressions and actions incorporate, transmit, and inform very ancient gestures.[11] According to the famous anecdote, Sraffa embarrassed Wittgenstein by asking him what the logical form was for the Italian gesture of rubbing one's chin with the index and middle finger to express indifference. Wittgenstein could have answered, following Bacon, that it was a transient hieroglyph, an expression whose origin had been forgotten and which, despite this, continued to exist in the social world. The same answer could be given about the origin of documents, and about that crucial document we call money.

From this purely analytical level one can draw a dialectic conclusion. In fact, the thesis that documentality is the necessary condition of the social world is first and foremost intended in a completely plain and ordinary sense: what people can do in terms of individual choices and undertakings is strongly conditioned by – if not completely dependent on – documents. Probably nobody has ever denied this, and yet, to my knowledge, no one has drawn from this the consequences concerning the foundations of social reality. Based on what we have seen so far, indeed, recording is what constitutes the true "power" of the social world.

9 In short, it is difficult to imagine Attila under house arrest for abuse of power. Which is a meager consolation: his empire, poor in documents, had the strength to arise (under the impulse of organized structures, like the fighting groups of Huns trained since childhood in the use of bow and horses and in coordinated action) but not to survive in the face of more documented organizations, such as the Eastern Roman Empire.

10 How many people know why we shake hands in greeting or agreement? And, a fortiori, how many children playing *Ring a Round the Rosy* ("*We all fall down*") are aware that they are probably recreating the epic collapse at the end of the Titanomachy?

11 Andrea de Jorio, *La mimica degli antichi investigata nel gestire napoletano*, Stamperia del Fibreno, Napoli, 1832.

2.3. *Sufficient condition*

I now come to the second part, properly dialectical, of social ontology. The point here is to prove that recording, of which documentality is the social manifestation qua recording of acts, constitutes not only the necessary but also the sufficient condition of social reality. *Recording and sentient individuals are enough for there to be social reality.* This is what allows for social codes, language, rituals, writing, and documents in the strict sense. This is what, at the phylogenetic level, determines the birth of meaning, conscience, and intentionality, with a development that is repeated at the ontogenetic level in the formative process by which each of us progressively gains access to consciousness and meaning through education and language. In short, it is true that documents alone do not speak, and need humans endowed with intentionality to talk. But it is equally obvious that only documentality – in a process that lasted hundreds of thousands of years and which originates in our animal past, starting with the first document act of marking the territory – has allowed for the genesis of consciousness and, within it, of intentionality. I would like to illustrate this thesis through five arguments that can be drawn from the reflection on the social world.

The argument of the ghost

My first argument is very simple, and I refer to "the ghost" in it because it merely claims that, by calling intentionality the foundation of documentality and the social world as a whole, one is resorting to an ontologically inconsistent function that is only manifested phenomenologically as a psychological experience – the impression of having will and understanding. Thus, documentality is the sufficient condition of social action because it undoubtedly works, whereas those who say that collective or individual intentionalities precede documentality – that is, that they are its sufficient condition – are merely flagging a ghost, and not really offering an alternative explanation. So, documentality is both a necessary and a sufficient condition, while intentionality is neither one nor the other. If this answer may seem trenchant and perhaps a bit weak, I invite the reader to relate to our most common experiences, as evidenced by the relationship between money and value. Since we rarely know the intrinsic value of things, most of the times, at the supermarket, we let ourselves be guided by value: we assume that the most expensive wine is the best, and therefore develop the intention to buy it. Even more so in the art market: the most expensive painting is the best, and therefore we develop the intention to praise it, if not to buy it. The core of the argument of the ghost is that postulating a transcendent and motivating intentionality as opposed to documentality – namely

evoking a ghost that turns on the machine – is not too different from postulating an intelligent design at the origin of the universe. There is no need for
it, and it complicates things that are indeed rather simple.

The argument of the cell phone

My second argument is indeed "at hand". At the time of landlines, one could
stay out of the house for hours. The phone would ring, but (unless one had
had the bad idea of getting voicemail) being "unreachable" was not something you could be blamed for. Now, as soon as you turn your phone back
on after a flight, you are invaded by dozens of emails, "missed calls", text
messages – a whole series of recorded acts that *arouse* responsibility. We
have to respond, and this duty often comes along with the malaise that ever
since Hegel has been attributed to consciousness. This proves that moral
upheaval originates from passivity, which is not necessarily in us. Therefore, intentionality, in all its forms (will, responsibility, conscience) comes
not from a simple representation – as it is usually said, mistakenly – but
from recording: from the fixation of the representation that allows for its
lasting duration and effectiveness. Indeed, documentality – and its fundamental principle: recording – are perfectly capable of producing such a
psychological upheaval – Aristotle's "movement" of the soul, which is trig-
gered whenever we turn on our cell phone. Which is even more evident if,
from the effects of recording on specific acts like being responsibilized by
the cell phone (or, conversely, being deresponsibilized when we "drink to
forget", as we readily admit) we move on to the formative action produced
by recording systems and archives like culture, language, tradition, and
education, which determine the genesis of individual intentionality.

Technical devices submit and mobilize us firstly because they are able to
generate individual responsibilities: we are called to *answer to*, under the
action of an appeal that is addressed to us individually and that is recorded
(that is, it is addressed to us and cannot be ignored). However, responding
passively is the source of *answering for*, responding in an active way, as
bearers of morality and freedom: insofar as humankind is educated to
the structure of answering-to it can later formulate the derived structure
of answering-for (that is, being morally responsible). Obviously, those
who transmit education can also do so intentionally (think of educators)
or simply give the example without being aware of having a pedagogical
function. What matters is that the intentionality (and responsibility) of
those who receive education or witness the example are not a primitive, but
a derivative, something that takes place a posteriori as the result of an
emergence. This takes me back to the thesis that it is not true that first we
have intentions and then they can be fixated in documents. The opposite is

true: first we are "trained" through documents (rituals, education), and only later this training can turn into intentionality. The modeling role played by the Homeric poems or the sacred texts underlie most social dynamics. The Crusades would hardly have been conceivable without the Bible and the Koran. The human being becomes such through an education that involves learning a language, rituals, and attitudes – i.e. document apparatuses that precede, not follow, the formation of conscience and moral responsibility. Indeed, no transformation could take place without a recording, without the establishment of a social memory, which later may generate an individual intentionality. This is initially sedimented into rituals, in external means for the fixating of memory in a society without writing. However, something like writing will soon form. For example, think of technical acquisitions, such as flintworking, a reification of memory in handwork; likewise, it does not seem accidental that very soon there should be rock paintings, which also represent a form of protodocumentality in this case. Indeed, as paleontologists suggest, rock paintings have a descriptive and a prescriptive value, just like our documents: they show where and how to hunt, or, for instance, what the sacred animals for the clan are.

With the development of writing, sociality evolves much more rapidly, social bonds and obligations become more complex, and the role of documents becomes more powerful (showing how they are constitutive of reality). Therefore, postulating intentionality before documentality means asking too much of the human being and denying evidence. You follow the rule (which you were given, and comes from the outside) before you understand it, and precisely through responsibilization an email – and the web in general – takes on a power akin to that of the state, tradition, taboos, and family. Responsibilization is the function of command. How does the command work? By responsibilization: you have received my message, I know you have received it (especially if you have WhatsApp: recently, a court sentence has made it a legitimate way to fire someone), everything is recorded, and you have to answer – otherwise it's as if you looked away from me, or from the other. By retorsion: if you don't answer, next time you need me I will not answer, and in the long run this will lead to civil death. By threat: if you don't answer, there are dozens (hundreds, thousands) of people who will. These virtual squabbles (unknowingly) echo the origin of moral instinct. Norms are transmitted through recordings (codes, rituals, which require recording for their formation and transmission) long before being understood.

The argument of the turtle

The third argument, that of the turtle, is particularly evident in the case of money. As we have seen, the question "what is money?" has a very simple answer: a document that is also accessible to illiterate people. But if the question were "what does this document depend on?" the answer would be "on other documents", with a regress that isn't infinite but goes back to the origins of humankind. The beginning of this lies in scenes where the distance between human and non-human animals diminishes, revealing the small gap between a wolf marking his territory and a Wall Street wolf activating a subprime system. I expect a sacrosanct objection: explaining documents through other documents is like arguing that the world is supported by an infinite series of turtles. But it isn't so. Because the pile of turtles is called to (improbably) explain a physical phenomenon, while the fact that documents depend on other documents is something that is part of our most ordinary experience. Indeed, our common experience is not that collective intentionality creates documentality. A municipal employee and I can very well agree on the absurdity of a procedure that makes us both waste much time: our shared intentions though are not enough to exempt us from the procedure – and its inventor would be hard to find, resulting from a stratification of which it is impossible to find the original act.

The argument of endless antiquities

My fourth argument is a development of the previous one. If one considers that the world – the same world in which species and society originated – is four and a half billion years old, and that life has existed for more than three billion years, then it will not be surprising that there was a long subconscious emergence originating the species as we know them but also writing, technology, documents, money, and gods. These institutions were already there when people started thinking about them and recognizing them as such, just as language was already there when consciousness was formed as a consequence of it and when people began to investigate the origin of language – often identified in a convention and a construction (the idea of language as a divine gift seems much more reasonable than this hypothesis, as it describes an emergence that takes place independently of consciousness). Even from this point of view the case of money is particularly instructive. It is difficult to conceive of money without reference to the notion of "writing", since the origin of money is the same as that of writing: small stones (*calculi*) or inscriptions that took account of trade even before the constitution of financial capital. So, there is one same long chain joining things like the fact that, hundreds of thousands of years ago, hominids noted the motion of the moon through the constellations, the birth of the first credit systems, the names of the gods, and of course the very stern divinity Mammon: money (indeed, all religions had to deal with it, at least trying to keep her as a good neighbor).

The argument of the pyramid

There is one final question: if everything, in the social and the psychic world, originates in stones and documents, notches, glyphs, and dusty papers, then how can we explain the evidence of phenomena like intentionality, will, and meaning? How can we deny them, considering the space they occupy in our psychological and social life? In agreement with what I have said about the relationship between the manifest structure and the deep structure of social reality, I have no intention of being a reductionist with regard to conscience, will, and intentionality. My only point is that they did not have an absolute beginning, but rather emerged – as should now be clear – from a document stratification. Take meaning, for example. The latter, just like value and money, emerges through technology and time – just as the pyramids, which for Hegel are the symbol of the sign, only manifest the long-lasting need to protect a tomb from desecration. Over the centuries, tombs evolved into masses of earth and stones, which have grown to give rise to pyramids (which, as a result, could only have the shape of a pile). When the pyramids were made, *then* we wondered "what does that mean?" and interpretation and signification began. Similarly, after finding a number of similar shells we decided to use them to count, to express meaning, and to determine values (if this argument seems unconvincing, consider that one who has just won a million euros is immediately confronted with an unusual and unexpected new question: "How will I spend it?" and with a new set of aspirations she had hitherto been unaware of).

2.4. Power and form

Thus far I have demonstrated (or at least I hope I have done so) that documentality is both the necessary and the sufficient condition of social reality. But social ontology does not simply include those forces that preside over the genesis of documents and the formation of intentionality. They also have a special force that jurists call "normativity" and philosophers call "power". Indeed, one can say that pieces of paper make us learn to read and write, or that rites teach us to exist in the world. However, what I want to investigate is rather the origin of the power that any kind of source (God, totem, taboo, piece of paper) exerts on individual intentionality. Answering this question leads us to the ultimate reason for the power of money, and for documents in general (which have more limited powers, while money generally has power over "everything that money can buy"). We have two traditional answers.

The first is openly Pentecostal: authority comes from the grace of God. The second is more likely, and is marked by a contractual nature: authority comes from the will of the nation, that is, in contemporary terms, from collective intentionality. Despite appearances, this second version is even more difficult to justify than the first (while being equally Pentecostal), because a decree of an occupying authority could cause a currency to be invalid, and the will of the nation could not in any way cause things to be otherwise. God's grace and the will of the nation are the mythological impersonations of a *legitimacy* which still does not explain the *efficacy* (the mystical foundation) of authority. As always, the emergentist hypothesis turns things around. Authority, normativity, the power of law (just like intentionality) do not precede documentality but result from it. The case of responsibility, which I addressed in the argument of the cell phone, might be a first answer, because responsibility is a normatively oriented attitude originating in recording. Norms and authority come from outside (and this externality is an essential part of their effectiveness), and impose actions that precede understanding by instituting canons, objectives, and rules.

It is not necessary to hypothesize the magic of the spirit behind the rise of normativity or intentionality. In both cases, before the spirit there is the letter. We have forms – letters, pyramids, totems, bulletins that are as obscure as totems, payment alerts, notifications, decrees, missed calls, unread emails, and then the clear document of a banknote. There is just one common trait to all these forms, but it is a crucial one: they are all recordings, fixating an act, from the simple missed call to the more solemn one of a bank emitting money or a parliament promulgating a law. This recording, in turn, will then evoke something like the spirit, generating reactions to the call, the purchasing power, or the law. In the best cases (as that of money) it will even create a (very concrete and not at all mystical) collective intentionality – the thing that makes us all obey the authority of the color of money. As said so far, though, it does not precede but follows the document.

3. Technology

As I said (and as I will try to demonstrate in this last section), technology guarantees the transition from ontology to epistemology and vice versa. In the case of the natural world, this transition takes place between ontology and epistemology, and I will not deal with it here.[12] In the case of the social world, instead – and in agreement with what has been said thus far – the interaction takes place from epistemology to ontology, from form to force. This is a crucial point, at the level of the deep structure, and I'm not the first

12 I have offered a speculative analysis of this interaction in Maurizio Ferraris, *Emergenza*, Einaudi, Torino, 2016.

to deal with it; in particular, the following is an attempt to give a clear form to some of Derrida's deep but obscure intuitions on speech acts, which had irritated Searle at the time.[13]

The idea is very simple: you cannot get married (or stipulate a contract, or make any social act) in just any way, but always according to a certain form. For example, at the wedding, you must answer "I do" and not "certainly" or "you bet". The illocutionary force of the act (ontology) is thus dependent on the form (epistemology) and it derives from the iteration of a ritual (the "due forms", that is, the forms that iterate a certain pattern thereby resulting *conform* to it). Note that it derives from iteration, not from understanding: I could be a civil law professor, and know everything about marriage, but I could not actually get married unless I repeated exactly the formula, that is, the codified form of the act. So, in social dynamics, there are not just two levels at stake, what we know and what there is, but three: what we know, what we do, and what there is. This third and very important level is precisely that of technology as *competence (know how) without understanding (know that) reinforced by iteration.* Let's look closer at this layer, which is often neglected but is the key to clarifying social reality and its riddles, starting with that of money.

3.1. Competence without understanding

Competence is a *praxis* that can result in a *poiesis*, a practical attitude that leads to a result: the bee makes honey, the termite builds the termite mound, Michelangelo sculpts Moses, Maradona scores goals. But *poiesis*, the more or less ritualized action, may also happen with no reason, as shown by people who knit, scrabble on a piece of paper, or play with their phone. Without hands, without the experience of handling and grasping, we would not have had thought; without manual competence (prehension) we would not have had understanding (comprehension).[14] Hands are prehensile; they grasp things (as Hegel knew very well, seeing the noun *Begriff*, "concept" as related to the verb *greifen*, "to grasp"). Hands indicate and, when they indicate without grasping, making gestures, they start the production of symbols. Technology, here, is not an alienating or dehumanizing principle, as in Pentecostal conceptions of intentionality. It is the origin of intentionality and conceptuality – without technology we would not have had money

---

13 Jacques Derrida, "*Signature, événement, contexte* (1971)"; id., *Marges de la philosophie*, Les Éditions de Minuit, Paris, 1972; id., "*La différance* (1968)", id., *Marges de la philosophie*, cit.

14 Cf. Colin McgGinn, *Prehension*, The MIT Press, Cambridge, MA, 2015 and the vast literature in Anaxagoras, Aristotle, Heidegger, and Derrida that I examine in *Where Are You?*, cit.

or computers, but most importantly we would not have felt the need for them either; it was the human accumulation of technical capabilities over hundreds of thousands of years (making humans such by the virtue of the resources and possibilities coming from their prostheses) that determined the pragmatic and semantic space creating the need for money, computers, institutions, and so forth.

Man (and woman) is not primarily a rational animal, nor is he a social animal (sociality seems to be an imposition, always precarious, dictated by evolutionary needs), but a technical animal who likes to use his hands – which is the only activity in which he excels compared to non-human animals – to keep himself entertained or to produce something. Neither the bee nor the termite nor Michelangelo nor Maradona could explain exactly what made them make a particular action. More importantly, even if Michelangelo or Maradona (let alone bees and termites) were able to explain their action, their explanation would not facilitate their performance in the future (it is possible that it would make it worse), nor would it help anyone replicate these actions (sculpting Moses or scoring goals), unless the explanation were accompanied by the practical repetition of certain acts. What matters is doing, not knowing.

This should not be surprising. Even in language, there can be competence without understanding, since I can correctly locate an object from its name (referential competence) without necessarily being able to locate it within a minimal epistemological landscape (inferential competence).[15] Indeed, the inferential dimension can also be seen as a "competence" that at least in some cases seems to be able to do without an "understanding". In this sense, Wittgenstein's motto "meaning is use" seems to suggest that meaning (both inferential and referential) is first of all a matter of competence (use) rather than understanding. What in the philosophical tradition has been called in many ways – such as schematism, transcendental imagination, dialectic, or *différance* – is a technological disposition that manifests itself from the most elementary apparatuses and then evolves into increasingly complex formations, such as a reproductive faculty that carries ontology into epistemology. Reciprocally, technology is not only related with the remote origins of man, but with the highest intellectual achievements: it shows in mathematics and logic, in the creation of scientific experiments and artistic works, in the actions and rituals that accompany our social life.

Art is a typical example of this competence without understanding. The artist does not know why he or she made the artwork exactly in that way (Leibniz's "nescio quid"): the work – as shown by the invocation to

---

15 Diego Marconi, *Lexical Competence*, The MIT Press, Cambridge, MA, 1997.

the goddess in the Homeric incipit – has always been conceived as the product of inspiration, coming from the outside and not controlled by the author. Most often the descriptions of the compositional process appeal to unconscious elements, or to an automation that guides the realization (the characters develop as if they were alive, certain words – for example "nevermore" in Poe's "Raven" – guide the whole composition). To stick to the artistic field, think of "formativity",[16] that is to say, the fact that artistic work finds its own rules while being in progress. This, however, is not restricted to art and applies to the technology in general, which on the one hand appears to be the realm of iterativity, but on the other hand is presented as the sphere of an inventiveness that is interesting precisely as it is not animated by any preliminary intentionality. No one could have foreseen from the outset the possible uses of the lever and the wheel (not to mention more complex devices). So, the functions that philosophers often attribute to a super-human faculty, imagination, should rather be attributed to the possibilities of recording, exteriorization, and accumulation that are immanent to technology.

Social interaction is another outstanding example of technology. The image of human action as an unconscious practice that becomes conscious only through a historical becoming (an image that goes from Vico to Hegel and historicalism) fully takes into account the deep structure. We do not know the reasons for our actions, and only sometimes can we explain them. Reciprocally, knowing the principles of our actions does not make us more efficient (otherwise, the professors of military academies would be the greatest strategists, which almost never happens). Coming to mathematics and seemingly more abstract forms of thought, it is worth noting that Euler argued that all the strength of his mathematics lay in the pencil he used, and Turing's great discovery was to understand that in order to calculate, it is not necessary to know what mathematics is, but it is necessary to have technical skills that allow for the calculation. How did Vico put it? *Homo non intelligendo fit omnia*: Humans act before they understand, and understanding, if and when it comes, it is not the premise (as the Cartesians think) but the result.[17] Following a powerful image proposed by Dennett,[18] compare a termite mound and the Sagrada Familia in Barcelona. They look the same, but how is it possible? Gaudi drew projects, he had representations; the

---

16 Luigi Pareyson, *Estetica. Teoria della formatività* (1950), Bompiani, Milano, 1989.

17 Giovan Battista Vico, *The New Science of Giambattista Vico: Unabridged Translation of the Third Edition (1744) With the Addition of "Practice of the New Science"*, Cornell University Press, Ithaca, 2016.

18 Daniel C. Dennett, *From Bacteria to Bach and Back: The Evolution of Minds*, Bradford Books and The MIT Press, Cambridge, MA, 2017.

termites had nothing of the sort. And yet, this is precisely the point: even Gaudi's neurons had no representations, they simply "downloaded", just like termites. After all, the latter found a shortcut: instead of creating representations, like Gaudi's neurons, they directly created the Sagrada Familia.

3.2. Iteration

Kant had rightly noted that to go from concepts (epistemology) to objects (ontology), it is necessary to have a medium term called "schema", characterized by a highly technological qualification – he spoke of schematism as "hidden technique" (*verborgene Kunst*, which usually translates as "hidden art", but whose meaning is obviously the same as "hidden technique"). However, conditioned by dualism and his "Pentecostal" attitude (which in this case is the idea of a priori with respect to experience), Kant described schematism as a process from the top to the bottom, while not excluding (and this is even clearer in the *Critique of Judgment*) a process from the bottom to the top, which for Kant is the subsumption of the objects of experience under categories. In this framework, the philosophy of technology turns out to be a "first philosophy", to the extent that it is in fact a "third philosophy", a philosophy that examines the medium between being ("firstness" to quote Peirce: ontology) and knowledge ("secondness", again in Peirce: epistemology).

If Peirce's triadic scheme is this (where the object constitutes the firstness, the sign is the secondness and the interpretant is the thirdness) (see Figure 2.2).

The perspective behind the theory I propose is shown in Figure 2.3.

Whatever is this thirdness? – some may object. Well, open your wallet, check your phone, and you'll see it. The economist Hernando de Soto has

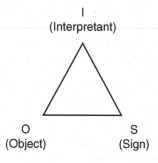

Figure 2.2 Peirce's triadic scheme

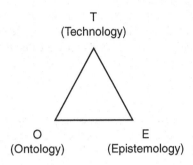

Figure 2.3 Documentality's triadic scheme

noted the importance of documents in the creation of wealth,[19] but two other points are worth considering. First, the role of documents is not limited (as de Soto claims) to fixating properties through records, therefore transforming them into marketable objects, but it constitutes the original cause of the production of financial wealth, inconceivable without documents. Roughly a century before de Soto, Oswald Spengler had already spoken of "Faustian money", that is, the money of finance "as Function, the value of which lies in its effect and not its mere existence",[20] first introduced by the Normans in England. To that, Spengler opposed, in a typecasting move, ancient money, or "money as magnitude". We could speak of synthetic money – money that produces new value (like capital) – while money as magnitude could be called analytic money, limited to the sphere of accounting. This function of money, with a singular anthropomorphism, in Searle is traced back to imagination.[21] But why attribute to a human faculty something that of course is neither conceived nor controlled by the human capacity of calculation and invention?

After all, I do not think it is a coincidence that every form of authority came with some technological innovation, which *preceded* it: the archive as the basis of legal power, the bank as the basis of capitalist power, and now documediality, marking the union between the constitutive power of documents and the mobilizing power of the media, which emerged thanks to the web.[22]

19 Hernando de Soto, *The Mystery of Capital: Why Capitalism Triumphs in the West and Fails Everywhere Else*, Basic Books, New York, NY, 2000.
20 Oswald Spengler, *Der Untergang des Abendlandes. Umrisse einer Morphologie der Weltgeschichte*, Verlag Braumüller, Wien, 1918.
21 John R. Searle, *Making the Social World*, cit.
22 Maurizio Ferraris, *Postverità e altri enigmi*, il Mulino, Bologna, 2017.

3.3. The mystic foundation of authority

Let me sum up and conclude. Do we give value to money? No, money (and, more generally, what I call "documentality") creates the notion of value itself. This explains why even an anarchist is reluctant to throw money out the window, and why a poor person tends to see herself as worthless (while a rich person tends to think the opposite). Searle sees money as deceitful, but only because his view of humankind is too flattering: for him, man is self-sufficient and invents money for practical reasons, only to be deceived by the artifice he himself created. For me, instead, without technology – and especially without the technologies of writing, culture and documents – man is not a perfect and philosophizing savage, but an unattractive animal destined to a "solitary, poor, nasty, brutish, and short" life, to use Hobbes's famous words. Indeed, ever since their first appearance, humans have developed technologies, perfected them, and little by little created sparks of history, conscience, and meaning. Money is no exception. If you try to imagine a world without money, you will have to imagine a world without ideas, art, spirit, or language. It is a full package; you cannot choose. The wiser thing to do is try to understand – understand that, for example, the process that led to the credit system is the same that generated the Bible, Shakespeare, and the Code Napoléon. So, for me the money is not a deceit but a riddle, just like religion. And this mystery (on which John and I have tried to shed some light) harbors what Pascal called "the mystical foundation of authority":[23] the power of things that have always been there, and that determine conscience much more than conscience (alone or with collective intentionality) could ever determine them. So, instead of thinking that money corrupts our soul, let us consider that without money (and the network of concepts it belongs to, which makes up social reality) we would have nothing to call a soul: nothing with which to pay our therapist, but nothing for her to cure either.

---

23 Pascal, *Pensées*, Ed. Brunschvicg, p. 294.

3 Socio-legal reality in the making

Money as a paradigm[1]

Angela Condello

1. A basic social institution

This chapter is the result of an analysis that cuts across the theses exposed by Searle and Ferraris, and it is – in some sense – also a synthesis of their philosophical systems. Furthermore, with this chapter I attempt to draw a connection between the hybridation of their theories of social ontology, on the one hand, and legal ontology, on the other hand. In order to do so, I shall argue that money as a unit of measurement shows relevant analogies with the social rules known as *laws*. Both money and those rules, in fact, are reflexive institutions: they exist in order to guarantee the peaceful coexistence of individuals within society, they do not exist in nature and are observer-dependent. Both, moreover, are valid inasmuch as they are posed and recorded according to conventional procedures. And both are normative: I can use this paper (a banknote) to pay for my train ticket, and I cannot use a page of the notebook here on my table – which is also a piece of paper, at an objective level – because they are different. The difference between these two pieces of paper lies at the bottom of Searle's and Ferraris's remarks, and is the core question concerning institutions.

Money, like law, can be considered as a *basic social institution*: its development shows, again, analogies with the evolution of law. First, the exhibition of certain rhythmic phenomena. From chaotic fortuitousness, as Simmel points out, money must have passed through a stage that at least reflects a principle and a meaningful form.[2] Thus, money gains a certain continuity in availability through which it can adjust itself to all objective and personal needs. Finally, it is objectified as a pure medium of transactions. But the passages are gradual.

---

1 This chapter is a reworked version and integration of my chapter in the Italian book *Il denaro e i suoi inganni*, entitled "La cornice e l'oggetto sociale simbolico. Il denaro tra intenzionalità e documentalità", Einaudi, Torino, 2018, pp. 109–126.
2 Georg Simmel, *The Philosophy of Money*, London and New York: Routledge, 2004, pp. 533–534.

The present chapter aims at situating money within a broader set of social institutions, together with law, and at defining their content as institutions in relation to the procedures of evaluation of conflicts (law) or balance of different interests (money) from which they are defined.

As pointed out in a recent work by Francesco Guala,[3] money is considered a fundamental economic institution, an institution that over the years has gained importance and has become the typical test or example in social ontology discourse. Like other institutions, such as the library I am working at in this moment, or the university where I teach, money creates powers and obligations and specifies the type of actions that *can, must*, or *must not* be performed in certain circumstances. Like law and like other social institutions, money involves questions and dilemmas related to cooperation.

What is money, then, and why is it created? The same questions could be asked for all institutions. What is marriage? Or, more broadly, what is law, and why is it created? A motto says "money is what money does", and in some sense this simple statement offers a synthetic idea of what I intend to claim in this chapter. In depicting the functionalist character of social institutions, Guala wrote:

> the notion of function is strictly related to the idea of purpose or goal. So what is the purpose of institutions? As a first approximation, it seems that institutions facilitate coordination and cooperation [. . .] Sometimes these collective activities are not particularly problematic, and coordination takes place easily. But at other times, the same goal can be achieved in different ways, each way implies a different division of labor, and it is not clear which is the best way to do it. In such cases, we shall say that there is a problem of coordination.

For institutions to work, there must be agreement about their nature and function, at a basic level; at a deeper level, people must be motivated to follow the rules that define the institutions. For money to be recognized and used as a medium of exchange, there must be a set of beliefs – in other words, its value must be backed by a system of beliefs and of procedures that give it value.

2. Overview on Searle's and Ferraris's theories of money

As it has hopefully become clear with the preceding chapters, and as it has been anticipated in the introduction, the double perspective presented in this monograph is aimed at trying to look at money in a different way. From this

---

3 Francesco Guala, *Understanding Institutions: The Science and Philosophy of Living Together*, Princeton University Press, Princeton, NJ, 2016, pp. xxii–xxiii.

perspective, money emerges as a tool that *works* through language while putting it into question, *operates* through social relations while defining them, and *shows* paradigmatically why and how a fundamental social fact like exchange works.

Searle discusses two strong theses. The first is that money is a matter of ordinary language. Like any form of exchange, it is a typically human thing, because no other animated being makes use of ordinary language as understood by Searle. Not only is this (language) a system of signs and meanings (which can certainly be found in many cases in the animal kingdom): it is also something capable of creating status functions. Social objects – like money – perform certain functions, and the functions exist in relation to the fact that we have assigned some kind of intentionality to the objects of these categories. The existence of these objects is relative to, and dependent on, both intentionality and the observer, whereas other objects exist independently of the observer. Mountains, trees, and molecules exist in a way that is not relative to the observer, while computers, cars, and pens exist in a way that is relative to the observer. The functions are always relative to the observer and are such because only the observer can attribute certain functions to the objects.

Searle's second thesis is based on the distinction between the level of objectivity and that of subjectivity (which he distinguishes into an *epistemic* level, relating to knowledge, and an *ontological* level, concerning existence). Money is an entity that exists only to the extent that something (ontology) is thought of *as* money (epistemology). The operation that allows for this attribution of value (epistemic level) to something (ontological level) can be applied to anything (a shell, a gold ingot, a can of beer, a pair of pants). And this is how the whole social reality is constructed: this operation, i.e. the attribution of a status function, is what makes it so that what is in the world (a piece of metal, a person in flesh and bones) is promoted to a socially relevant level by being collectively recognized *as* something relevant (a coin, a husband, a professor, or a finance officer). Status functions are important because they attribute power over others. However, Searle does not explain *how* they attribute power, despite he suggests that power, in his opinion, derives from the persistence of these functions, thus from a temporal level that he nevertheless does not deepen.

Once an object is treated *as* a coin, it cannot stop being used that way just because collective intentionality shifts that value to another object, such as a hat. If a man is a husband, for him to cease being such it is necessary to go through a long (and painful) bureaucratic procedure made of registers, archives, files, and signatures: in other words, it is necessary to go through the documental system that until then has ensured the persistence of that status. This is a sort of material, physical, and traceable mark of the intention expressed on the wedding day ("I do", in the sense of "I have pictured it", "I understand it", according to the most complete meaning of intentionality).

The Latin term *status*, in my opinion, is the first element linking Searle's and Ferraris's theories: it must be understood in the sense of *remaining* firm, *sticking* to a position, and *keeping* balance. The intentional dimension, central to the thought of the American philosopher, has to be very solid for the function of money not to be ephemeral, that is, for money to be more than barter (a sort of peer to peer exchange, a possible ancestor of bitcoin). Money as a status function is created through the constitutive rule "X counts as Y in C": the object X acquires the function, the exchange value Y, within the context C. This constitutive rule provides reasons to act and conditions our desires regardless of our inclinations.

In his chapter, Ferraris explains how this intentional attribution of value to objects can be possible. While acknowledging the importance of intentionality in the philosophy of money and in social ontology as a whole, he investigates *how* money is able to mobilize us (and not just *why*, as Searle does). The result is that both of these readings place money at the center of our society because money is a paradigm of its functioning: it increases our power because beyond the form of the object (the coin, the banknote, but also more broadly the bank account, the bank itself, and so on – up to the International Monetary Fund) there is the force of the object. Money is an allegory of human bonds, even though it exists independently from the dimension of the bond in the traditional legal sense. This allegory incorporates the exchange of exchanges and therefore, at a closer look, it symbolizes the whole society.

Like Searle, Ferraris also reveals something, solving some puzzles concealed in what he defines the "deep structure" of social reality. Actually, in this case, rather than something that seems to be what it is not (deceit), this is something we are just not used to thinking about, or at least not enough. The deep structure is a system of recordings: a network of documents directly related to intentionality but, according to Ferraris, prior to it. Otherwise, he claims, the great financial crises of history could not be explained. If intentionality preceded documentality in time and importance, great depressions would have been avoided by shifting collective intentionality onto another object. The intermediate conclusion is that there must be a further system of elements in the construction of social reality for functions, values, and status to be able to persist and have a recognizable value over time.

Thus, Ferraris clarifies how the mystical foundation of the deontic power mentioned by Searle cannot be (only) collective intentionality. It certainly cannot be the prime foundation of the value of money and of all the things that, by virtue of their value, make us act. I intend to demonstrate that the foundation of the deontic power of money lies in the transition from an object's regular function (whatever it is) to its status function: the object, thanks to the status function, is registered *as* an object valid for exchange. *Inscription* is therefore a core in which the intention coincides with the trace, and only a new trace can modify it. The element of mysticism emerging from the idea of deontic power mentioned by Searle lies in identifying the origin of that power with an almost transcendent force: something makes us act through money, but it is still unclear *what*. The element of mysticism is revealed in Ferraris's theory.

From my perspective, then, money exists in between the two positions. This is also confirmed by Searle's constant reference to the necessary representation of the status function, without which the function would not take place nor could persist over time. Searle admits that the bank keeps a register, whose only physical form lies in the magnetic traces on the computer disks recording the amount of money one owns in the bank. Therefore, changes in the amount of money owned consist entirely of changes in its representation on the computer disks. Without things being fixated in a representation (which can be an inscription, a sign, a trace) and without a documental system that organizes the exchanges, the function of money, both in use and in trade, could not persist.

The imaginary debate between Searle and Ferraris must be situated within a broader field of money theories, developed by economists, philosophers, anthropologists. These are classified in two grand categories, called *commodity* and *claim* theories. Commodity theories of money go back to the work of Karl Menger, one of the pioneers of the marginalist approach that still constitutes the bulk of contemporary economics.[4] The famous essay published by Karl Menger in the *Economic Journal* (1892) constituted a historical reconstruction of the emergence of money *as a social institution*. According to Menger, this emergence was articulated in four steps:

1   Within a society characterized by the division of labor, there could be problems of *double coincidence of wants*: first, individuals specialize in the production of certain goods. Then, they might need some goods and not others. This imperfect coincidence of wants and desires leads to the search for a *medium of exchange* – i.e. to the search of a good that can be circulated and exchanged with the goods and commodities that one really needs.

2   So, at the beginning of such a process a single medium usually tends to emerge to facilitate the exchange: a good medium for the exchange

---

4 Francesco Guala, *Understanding Institutions*, cit., p. 36.

has to be portable, durable, and divisible. This is how money gradually emerges.

3   Then, the physical commodity that has emerged as a medium of exchange is likely to be replaced with certificates or other objects that are easily portable and can circulate. What originally was a concrete medium of exchange changes into an abstract medium of exchange.

4   The fourth – and final – step is a passage from concreteness to abstraction. Gold, or the other valuable and portable good, is replaced by *fiat* money, or *currency* money. The way it works is not particularly complex, at least superficially: the central banks keep issuing certificates but these certificates no longer grant the ownership of a certain amount of gold, since they only refer to an abstract currency. This kind of money has no value in itself: it can be used to purchase goods they might need or desire in the future. They trust, or believe (what Searle calls a "fantasy"), that other people will accept *that* money in the future – so money is a social phenomenon based on a complex system of mutual trust. Trust is necessary to back up the passage from the exchange of material commodities to the exchange of paper certificates which do not have any value in themselves and whose value is thus the result of a purely abstract process.

The main opponent theory of the commodity theory is known as *claim theory* (or state theory): according to this theory, money is created and sustained by state authority. For this mechanism to work, the state's credibility as a source of power must be solid. Guala writes:[5]

> If the state is shaky, it may not be in my interest to hold any fiat money: in six months' time there may be another authority in place, asking me to pay taxes by means of another currency. Notice that the state must also be a credible supervisor of the quantity and quality of money. Politicians may be tempted to print an increasing quantity of money to buy civil servants. But if the latter do not produce enough commodities and services, the flood of vouchers will generate inflation. Inflation in turn discourages people from holding currency, and in the long run may cause the entire monetary system to collapse. Only a strong, stable, and serious state can back up the system of self-sustaining beliefs with enough credibility to make a fiat currency viable.

Both *commodity* and *claim* theory emphasize the role of mutually consistent beliefs and, at the same time, both entail an equilibrium among

---

5 Francesco Guala, *Understanding Institutions*, cit., p. 40.

the individuals of a community – an incentive to use a currency provided that the others do the same. If the theory of commodity money might be explained by Searle's idea of a collective intentionality attributing value and power to certain objects and authorities, yet that part of the explanation remains incomplete without the complementary philosophical account on what fixes that collective intentionality.

The inscription – that enables the status function to exist and persist and that keeps it valid for the object-money – unites two elements: the concrete material object and its transcendent value. The power of money is deposited in the relationship between individual intentionality, collective intentionality, and documentality: this power has a symbolic root. The intention to establish a status function in that object is fixated by the inscription and by the collective recognition of that object as money. The coin, the banknote, the trace on the bank account are individual instances repeated an incalculable number of times, and yet every single time they are more than a piece of iron, a simple piece of paper, or a set of data in computer memory. More precisely, a coin is both a simple piece of iron and the value of use and exchange that transcends it. The latter is based on collective intentionality and on the need for it to be fixated on repeatable recording systems (iteration is one of the characters on which Ferraris rightly insists).

These philosophical arguments consider money as a usable good, one that has value according to its numerical indication: it does not matter to have this or that banknote in your pocket, but to have one that has *that* value. In Roman law the usable goods are *res quae pondere, numero, mensura consistunt*: those that can be easily replaced with others, as they have the same quantitative and qualitative structures. Their fungibility, however, always falls within a genre, a group whose limit is defined and known. The fixation of this defining limit occurs on the dual level of documentality and intentionality. The ontological dimension intersects the epistemological one in an ambiguity that can be found in money and in many other objects: according to Ferraris, bitcoin appear to be the most concrete form of money, as they are simple silicon recordings. The intangible concreteness of the bitcoin is given by its recognizability as a social object that is constituted as a *symbolon*, an amulet in which the individual instance coexists with the value to which it refers. It is a symbolic and reproducible social object, which is based on a document basis animated by collective intentionality.

In this symbolic foundation, money refers to the system of norms that hold society together: the deontic power of money and of norms cannot be self-founded, but needs a foundation.[6] Ferraris notes that collective

6 Gustavo Zagrebelsky, *Simboli al potere*, Einaudi, Torino, 2012.

intentionality is nothing more than a fiction by which we can say that every gesture, every decision and action, is not arbitrary or subjective, but belongs to a network of relationships and reciprocal recognition among subjects. For this reason, once again, money is first and foremost a power: owning it allows one to create potential constraints where they do not already exist. This potential obligation to others and to another collectivity, which we may call "society", is what makes us act in the respect of rules and what makes us recognize a given object as currency and a given individual as the President of the United States.

The peculiarity of money is that any recording (but not any volatile object) could be money, as Searle notes, but not all objects are used as money, as Ferraris notes. The recording (and therefore the fact of coming into existence) and the iteration of money have meant that it has slowly become a technically defined object, produced only in some places and in some ways; it can also be transferred virtually, but always through some very precise means. So, money is a *unicum*, so to speak: being the outcome of iteration, it can be found anywhere, but is it an individual object bearing a universal and widespread value.

Money is a paradigmatic social object because it is "a place of referral that presupposes a double layer of reality: one that lies beyond the factual and logical-demonstrative experience, which is, as it were, hidden behind a veil, and the one that the veil itself shows us, in the approximation [. . .] of disclosure and concealment".[7] Like any symbolic object, it is also intrinsically enigmatic and deceptive, because not everything about money can be understood through perception, and because what intuitively seems clear may be wrong – as Searle rightly notes in his analytic deconstruction. In every banknote in our wallet, there is a form (the visible one, the image) and a force (the invisible one, the theme or the content). For this dual nature, money is a symbolic social object that responsibilizes us and creates power.

In his seminal work on money, which has proven able to constitute a total philosophy, Simmel claims that "the unique significance [of] exchange [appears] as the economic-historical realization of the relativity of things [. . .]. No matter how closely the inner nature of an object is investigated, it will not reveal economic value which resides exclusively in the reciprocal relationship arising between several objects on the basis of their nature. Each of these relations conditions the other and reciprocates the significance which it receives from the other".[8] It is a relation of reciprocity

---

7 Gustavo Zagrebelsky, *Simboli al potere*, my translation, p. 6.
8 Georg Simmel, *The Philosophy of Money*, cit., p. 99.

that, without simplifying them, connects documentality and intentionality. Money should thus be brought back where it truly belongs: to the field of the theory of *exchange* – and therefore to the origin of human relations and of the system of social objects that surround us, affecting us aesthetically and intellectually, from the color of money to the theological matrix of the trust we have in it.

3. Social reality and law: cross-breeding intentionality with documentality

As already mentioned in the introduction, social ontology is a field of knowledge structured on complex sets of questions that touch upon different fields of research: how can social entities exist? What gives power to a head of state? What system of notions explains social and especially institutional reality? By going back, once again, to the theories presented by Searle and Ferraris, the following paragraphs aim at building a cross-disciplinary discourse on social and legal reality, taking into consideration both the classic philosophical analysis drawing especially on Searle and Maurizio Ferraris, as well as works on legal objects developed by legal historians and theorists, in particular by Yan Thomas and Aldo Schiavone.

On the one hand, reflections on the nature of social objects such as contracts, municipalities, money, and marriage have been discussed by philosophers since – to say the least – the linguistic turn, especially starting from Austin's theories on speech acts and on the performative character of language, that allows us to do things with words;[9] on the other hand, social scientists and in particular legal theorists have been interested in the relationship between the use of language and the production of institutional reality since antiquity.

While translating Searle's essay for the Italian version of the present project, I noticed that all of the examples he mentioned – apart from money – were of a specific type of "social" reality, which is what he calls "institutional" reality, and which can definitely be categorized as "legal" reality. The social objects he mentions – obligations, promises, money, marriage, legal statuses such as professorships – all fall within the category of legal reality if one was to observe reality from a legal-institutionalist point of view. The argument I intend to develop is that – however formalized – those objects exist inasmuch as there is an interest that needs social recognition, legitimation, and protection. Furthermore,

---

9 See in particular John Langshaw Austin, *How to Do Things With Words*, Harvard University Press, Cambridge, MA, 1962, and John Rogers Searle, *Speech Acts: An Essay in the Philosophy of Language*, Cambridge University Press, Cambridge, 1969.

in many of his works, also Ferraris recognizes that law is the paradigmatic field of study for social ontology. This hybridization between the social and the legal is a specific characteristic of debates on ontology of society: indeed, among the sea of social objects, it is actually hard to distinguish between what Searle and Ferraris refer to as "social objects", on the one hand, and those objects that would fall within legal reality, on the other. As aforementioned, besides money, the typical examples mentioned by the two philosophers include: property, marriage, or legal statuses such as being the mayor of a town.

From the perspective of legal theory, all reality can appear as *legal* reality: the typical distinction between *brute* facts and *institutional* facts, for the lawyer, is just a matter of taxonomy. Indeed, all nature can be juridified and it is processes through processes of juridification[10] that we regulate and define reality. The comparison between Searle's and Ferraris's accounts shall thus serve as a pretext to broaden the perspective on this set of issues, by considering money as a paradigmatic legal object to approach the very nature and essence of legal reality. Starting from the phenomenology of pecuniary exchange, I shall draw on Yan Thomas and Aldo Schiavone, both Roman law scholars, to dig into the historicity of legal ontology and on the very core of legal objects.

As aforementioned, Searle claims that money has value and gives us power because, collectively, we recognize that a piece of paper is valuable and it can be used in order to buy things. Ferraris, on the contrary, connects the value of money to the recording that backs the value – for this reason, he considers bitcoin basically constituted by recording – as an exemplary case of the contemporary socio-legal object: because they are *pure traces*. There is a basic disagreement between their perspectives: one roots socio-legal reality on intentionality (Searle), the other on documentality (Ferraris). Yet, what appears to be a divergence might constitute, in the tradition of legal history, a strong convergence (as I argue in §4 and §5). Here, I shall try to present my thesis about the convergence between intentionality and documentality by drawing on the works of two legal historians and theorists.

In two works of recent re-publication,[11] one on the value of things and the other on legal fictions, legal historian Yan Thomas has argued about

---

10 See on this Mariano Croce, *The Politics of Juridification*, Routledge, London, 2018.
11 Yan Thomas (2002), *Il valore delle cose*, ed. by Michele Spanò and with essays by G. Agamben and M. Spanò, Quodlibet, 2015; id. (1995), *Fictio legis*, ed. by Michele Spanò and with and essay by Michele Spanò and Massimo Vallerani, Quodlibet, 2016. On page 89, 93 and 94 of *Il valore delle cose*, Yan Thomas argues that all practices of denomination and all legal taxonomies relate to the process of the dispute and to the objective of its resolution; the *res* (thing, object) reflects the *lis* (dispute) and this actually shows the

the intrinsic connection between law, the performative force of language (which proves the thematic familiarity with the ontology of John Searle), and the importance of procedures (what Ferraris would call "technology") in the definition of social reality. Yet, Thomas questions the reasons of such a use of language and he claims that law uses language to create reality for the necessity to prevent conflicts. Such a perspective, that looks at legal procedures as the moment of main edification of the legal world, shows the validity of both the intentional and the documental theses, which interact within the process of "making" the legal world (paraphrasing Searle's *Making the Social World: The Structure of Human Civilization*, 2009). Beyond the opposition between the world of objects (or brute facts, or mountains, rivers, and bricks) and the world of subjects (who then create national parks and buildings), Thomas suggests a procedural and substantialist idea of permanent construction and redefinition of the legal world (in other terms: a "legal reality in the making").

If one looks at social reality through the lens of social ontology as it is usually approached by philosophers, the question is whether objects exist because they are considered to be objects (Searle) or if they emerge as such through a system of traceability and recordings (Ferraris). If one, instead, tries to look at the convergence of these two theories, the paradigm of legal construction of reality might emerge as the space of intersection between intentionality and documentality.

3.1. The symbolic socio-legal object for Searle: money as status function

Everyone who has familiarity with Searle's works knows that he usually starts his papers, arguments, and lectures on social ontology – or on the construction of social reality – from the example of money. Before a lecture, he would typically put his hand into his pocket, to then show his wallet, and subsequently a $20 bill. After this gesture, he typically asks his audience: "Why do we attribute meaning to this piece of paper?" "What characteristics of this piece of paper give me the power to buy goods through it?" In Searle's works, money constitutes a paradigmatic example of how social reality works. The reason is not, however, that a banknote is simply a more evident object that can be easily shown during a lecture, a tangible and material presence that each of us uses almost

---

identification between the legal *thing* and the *process* that makes it a thing legally relevant. The procedure is what keeps together speech acts and institutions – social competence and linguistic performance. This might explain why all the main works in social ontology mention examples chosen from the legal field.

(if not) every day. The reason is, following Yan Thomas and Schiavone, that money is a paradigmatic object because it is the concretization of the social exchange and is the measure of economic value, on which juridification is based.

But let us first go back to Searle's argument, that I will compare again to Ferraris's argument on the documental nature of socio-legal reality. To begin, the reason why money is among Searle's exemplary social objects is certainly that it constitutes the cornerstone of oppositions like concretion vs. abstraction, personal vs. impersonal, and it thus concerns, at the same time, human relationships *and* the function played by the regulation of those relationships. Money is a both a symbol and a reification of sociolegal reality. As suggested by Georg Simmel in *The Philosophy of Money*,[12] such an object shows the surface level of economic and human affairs, and it touches upon those fortuitous phenomena that characterize the life of humans within a regulated society. It is tiny, it circulates, and it is functional: there would be no money if there was no need to regulate and concretely conclude bargains or exchanges. Moreover, and most importantly, Searle claims that money is backed by a system of collective agreements on its value. Yet, I add, if there was no recording of those agreements, no valid documentation about exchanges, it would be hard to attribute *value* to objects: so, money is crucial because it shows the surface and the roots of social exchange and because it regards the normative character of such a bond. If one observes money more closely, it will become clear that it is not exceptional if compared to other objects created and regulated by law – and it actually has many similarities with law. Inasmuch as those objects, in fact, money is first and foremost a tool through which different actions can be achieved: it *works* through language while putting it into question, it *operates* through social relations while defining them, and it *shows* paradigmatically why and how exchange works. Simply, we tend to relate money to exchange and value-attributing processes more frequently than other objects such as property.

Searle's claim is that is a crucial social object from the perspective of philosophy first and foremost because it is based on a series of *deceptions*; thus, money is a perfect example of the linguistic construction of social reality because – as Yan Thomas would say about legal objects – it is a *fiction* that produces consequences on our life. A fiction with powerful consequences: the banknote, indeed, attributes powers. As anticipated, for Searle the explanation of such a power must be traced back to the human use of language. Thus, the answer to the question "What is it that makes

---

12 Georg Simmel, *The Philosophy of Money*, cit.

the piece of paper a banknote?" is: language. As he often stated, on issues concerning social reality, there is no way to escape ordinary language. As it clearly emerges from his most recurrent arguments, there is a sense in which most philosophy is ordinary language philosophy and, without any doubt, social ontology could be all traced back (and explained through) philosophy of language. Language is considered crucial by Searle because it is *through* language that we attribute a status function to a banknote, and so it is through language that the difference between a mere piece of paper and a banknote is produced.

In order to understand what he means by "status function", we should think of the typical examples of socio-legal objects that surround us: a public library, a taxpayer, etc. Human beings have the capacity to create a reality of *power relations* which exist only because they are believed to exist. Those power relations arise from the fact that a certain person or object has been assigned a certain status and with that status a function has been assigned – specifically, a function that can only be performed in virtue of the collective acceptance of that status. Searle thus explains money through the basics of his structure of human civilization: animals are not capable of attributing functions to objects because they lack representation (as far as we know): to get from pair, to bonding, to marriage, there must be a concept of "marriage", i.e. a way of representing two people as spouses, as husband and wife. This is a specificity of human civilization and, according to Searle, it is also a direct consequence of the performative power of language. Private property, government, universities, summer vacations, and cocktail parties – all these socio-legal objects are status functions in this respect. The reason to use language in such a way, Searle adds, is that it gives us power: we have rights and duties because of the status functions. Also, and more importantly, those rights and duties are independent of the inclinations or of the desires and feelings of the agents: that is to say, they are normative. In this sense, status functions are relevant inasmuch as they are normative. Here, again, I see a point of convergence between the analytic social ontology of John Searle and the idea – developed by Yan Thomas – according to which legal objects exist because there are conflicts, and thus because there are interests to protect.

Within his system of beliefs, Searle preserves the distinction between the linguistic process that creates the object and the status function; in other words, he maintains the process and the result separated. Yan Thomas, on the other hand, invites us to consider the continuity between these two poles, and in fact he insists on the essential correspondence between confusion and identity, as well as between dispute and process and name and object. From

Thomas's view, there is no point in distinguishing between *brute* and *institutional* facts (as Searle does, when claiming that "the object in his hand is composed of cellulose fibers" is a brute fact).

The observation of Searle's theoretical system through the lens of the law suggests to develop a more "oblique" idea of the relationship between language and legal reality.[13] From this perspective, as further remarks on Thomas and Schiavone will hopefully show, the distinction between those features of reality that exist regardless of what anybody thinks and those whose existence is dependent on our attitude – becomes a mere theoretical taxonomy, with weak relevance at the pragmatic level described by legal historians and theorists. Similarly, the distinction between entities that are observer (or mind) independent and those that are observer dependent (or observer relative) becomes, from the legal perspective, a mere categorization of definitions that help explain a system of thought. On the one hand, Searle lists typical examples of observer (or mind) independent objects, such as mountains, molecules, and galaxies. On the other hand, he lists objects which are mind dependent, such as money, private property, government, and marriage. These entities exist only relative to human attitudes. They are not observer independent, they are observer relative or observer dependent. Thus, money exists only insofar as something is thought to be money: it is observer dependent. However, from the perspective of legal theory that remains a descriptive claim: *why* is money observer dependent? The answer to this question entails the connection with Maurizio Ferraris's philosophy of documentality, on the one hand, and with remarks made from the very origins of the socio-legal world, on the other. Such a series of remarks shall be discussed in the third and concluding chapter of the present book.

To sum up, according to Searle, social reality is constructed through a series of passages: first, through language and collective intentionality we create status functions; this operation is what makes it so that what is in the world (a piece of metal, a person in flesh and bones) is promoted to a socially relevant level by being collectively recognized *as* something relevant (a coin, a husband, a professor, or a finance officer). Status functions are important because they attribute power over others. However, Searle does not explain *how* they attribute power, although he suggests that power, in his opinion, derives from the persistence of these functions.

---

13 Mariano Croce speaks of the obliquity of law in *The Politics of Juridification*, cit., especially on p. 1 and following.

3.2. *Tracing socio-legal reality: Maurizio Ferraris's documentality*[14]

When trying to explain why money is an exemplary social entity, Ferraris introduces another question, similar to that posed by Searle: "Which came first, money or the value we attribute to it?" When answering this question, Ferraris distinguishes two different levels of the discussion: a *surface* level, on which it might appear that the value of money precedes the object (for instance, the piece of matter constituting a coin or banknote); and a *hidden*, more profound level, where it is money that determines the value. The two poles around which the problem of the value of a banknote oscillates are objectivity and subjectivity. In order to avoid the circularity of the question ("What comes first?" – which resembles the chicken and the egg problem), Ferraris adds that money should be explained through the non-manifest or deeper level, that is to say it should be explained starting from the level where it is money that determines the value (and not vice versa). The underlying idea, or non-manifest level, of his theory is that we come into contact with the ontological dimension of the social world – that is, with the social forces (obligation, responsibility, motivation, intentionality) – not through understanding or knowledge (epistemology), but through action. When we handle money, first and foremost, we *act*: we *make* something together with other subjects. When we use money, we collaborate.

In some sense, Ferraris seems to have more familiarity with the proceduralist and substantialist thesis developed by Yan Thomas about the value of things. Ferraris explains the transition from the level of objects (such as money) to the level of knowledge (such as what we know about money, i.e. the ideas on why and how it gains its value) through an intermediate level, which he defines as "technology". *How* socio-legal reality functions and how it is enacted are the core questions that must be addressed theoretically to understand money. In this sense, Ferraris confirms the typical remarks about the rituality of the constructivist character of the law made by legal historians, according to whom linguistic forms constructed the legal world: for instance, he explains, we cannot get married (or stipulate a contract, or make any social act) in just any way, but we can do so only according to a certain *formula*. For example, at the wedding, we answer "I do", and not "Sure, great". What Austin and Searle had called the *illocutionary force* of the act (ontology), thus, depends on

---

14 Ferraris has developed his theory of documentality in various steps: in particular, the roots of his theory can be detected in *Estetica razionale* (Cortina 1997; 2011). His main work in the field is *Documentality. Why It Is Necessary to Leave Traces*, It. first ed. 2009; transl. by Richard Davies, Fordham University Press, New York, NY, 2012.

the form (epistemology) and derives from the iteration of form (in Roman law: *formula*) of a ritual.

Unlike Searle, Ferraris attributes the force of such an illocutionary act (such as "I do", or "I swear", or "I promise") not to the fact that we collectively and consciously accept the value of that utterance, but to the mere repetition, or iteration of the utterance. The *formula* which is uttered is the basic technology of socio-legal reality, in this sense. Therefore, he claims, in socio-legal reality there are not just two levels at stake – what we know (epistemology) and what there is (entities, ontology) – but three: what we know, what there is, and what we do (technology). Technology mediates between beings (ontology) and knowledge (epistemology).

What gives value to money is thus the technology through which the value is recorded – thus it is the documental nature of money (just like for other socio-legal objects) that gives it value and force. Without technology – and especially without the technologies of writing, archiving, and documenting – man would not be a perfect and philosophizing savage, but an unattractive animal destined to a lonely, poor, shameful, brutal, and short life.

To sum up, Ferraris explains how Searle's social ontology is possible, and how it works more concretely. Both philosophers place money at the center of our society because money is a paradigm of its functioning: it increases our power because beyond the form of the object there is the force of the object. The deep structure is a system of recordings: a network of documents directly related to intentionality but, according to Ferraris, prior to it. Otherwise, he claims, the great financial crises of history could not be explained. If intentionality preceded documentality in time and importance, great depressions would have been avoided by shifting collective intentionality onto another object.

The (not so) mystical foundation of deontic power mentioned by Searle cannot be (just) collective intentionality. It certainly cannot be the prime foundation of the value of money and of all the things that, by virtue of their value, make us act. The explanation of the deontic power of money is generated by the transition from an object's regular function (whatever it is) to its status function. The object, thanks to the status function, is *recorded as* a means of exchange. The inscription, or recording, that enables the status function and keeps it valid for the object – money – integrates both the concrete material object and its transcendent value. The power of money is deposited in the relationship between individual intentionality, collective intentionality, and documentality. And the essence of such a socio-legal object is its use, its capacity to function as a means to measure the value of interests at stake in a conflict, in a negotiation, in a transaction. The intention to establish a status function in that object is fixed by the inscription and by the collective recognition of that object *as* money. The coin, the banknote, the trace on the bank account are individual instances repeated an incalculable number of times, and yet every single time they are more than a piece of iron, a simple piece of paper, or a set of data in computer memory. More precisely, a coin is both a simple piece of iron and the value of use and exchange that transcends it. The latter is based on collective intentionality and on the need for it to be fixed on systems of recording (iteration is one of the characters on which Ferraris rightly insists).

The ontological dimension intersects obliquely the epistemological one in an ambiguity that can be found in money and in many other objects. The intangible concreteness of the bitcoin, for instance, is given by its recognizability as a social object that is constituted as a symbolon, a reproducible social object, which is based on a documental matter empowered by agreement and collective intentionality.

The peculiarity of money is that although any recording (but not any volatile object) could be money, as Searle notes, not all objects are used as money, as Ferraris notes.

Things are, in the end, what the dispute decides that things are: Yan Thomas reports that in Roman law, the term *pecunia* was often used to refer to the objects (*res*), be them promises, or contracts, or any other object with legal value. Pecunia would thus indicate the engagement in an exchange, more generally. It would indicate, in other words, things in themselves.[15]

4. Broadening the field: from money to legal reality

If the term *pecunia* was often used as a synonym to *res*, it is no surprise that contemporary philosophy (as proved by the works of Searle and Ferraris) often uses money as a paradigmatic socio-legal object. Also, this interchangeability invites a reflection on legal reality more generally. In order to understand legal objects and legal reality from an ontological point of view, we should question the reasons of their existence, as Yan Thomas suggests. If there is a point in distinguishing between the world of brute facts and the world of institutional facts, it is that such a distinction clarifies that – whereas mountains would exist independently from our will – money would not. Legal reality is, unlike brute reality, dependent on the *artifex*; it is artificial. It is posed by subjects (singular or plural), and described through language (as Searle explains perfectly). All legal reality is, to this extent, technological – if we focus on the meaning of the Greek root *tèchne*, which is correspondent to the Latin *ars* (from which *artificium*, artificial).

---

15 Yan Thomas, *Il valore delle cose*, cit., p. 15 ff.

Legal reality is constantly *in the making*, since it is the use we make of legal entities (such as through the statuses we attach to them) that explains their existence.

The juridification of the world is a process that makes things happen; things that, otherwise, would not happen: the favorite field of examples of Searle is law precisely because, without language and artificiality, legal reality would not exist. In a recent work on the politics of juridification, Mariano Croce writes:

> law claims to re-order things, to remould the order in which they are assembled. This is because the law is first and foremost a technique of description that provides guidance for conduct.[16]

The operational mode of the law is one that Croce calls "obliquity": legal technique is oblique, since it describes and it prescribes at the same time, and by recognizing some objects (relations, promises, etc.) it excludes others. In this sense, law is to be conceived as a performative force does not address the object directly, but affects it obliquely, by attending to something else. Legal taxonomies have accompanied the history of legal reality since its very origin: Yan Thomas reports that Roman lawyers were, in fact, concerned with the taxonomy of sacred, religious, and public things (*res*).

4.1. Res, pecunia, lis

The juridification of the world is thus an artificial process that involves both intentionality and documentality and that is based on the function of the entities that are constructed. Legal language drags a particular object within the legal sphere, or it constructs an object *ex novo* (for instance: a marriage) and by doing this a whole set of consequences is produced also outside of the field of action of that specific object. All this is possible because of the use of legal techniques (which were rituals in ancient law, and which are procedures in contemporary law). Procedures fix the substance of what falls into the regulatory scope of the law, and it is only through such technologies that legal words can determine the boundaries of what is legal and of what is non-legal. The *res* that make up legal reality show the essence of law and show why law is necessary. Legal reality is a sphere where both legal entities and what Searle would call "brute facts" interplay and are permanently redefined by means of a circular movement that involves all legal reality. Yet, legal reality is not just a matter of constructing the world through words

---

16 Mariano Croce, *The Politics of Juridification*, cit., p. 2.

(or, basically, of "making" the world): it is, instead, a way of approaching reality – an independent account of facts and events with enforceable effects on society.

Yan Thomas, in many of his works on Roman law, underlines the constructivist and proceduralist character of law: the legal knowledge is first and foremost a web of special signs that allow us to frame in legal terms those questions that people in everyday life verbalize with recourse to ordinary language (Searle) and solve with the normative resources of other (non-legal) rule-governed contexts.

This legal technology depends on who, how, when, and why is motivated to use legal instruments and for what purposes: this is why law shows the inevitable interconnection between intentionality and documentality, and not their mutual exclusion.[17] As noted by Agamben in the preface to Yan Thomas's work on the value of things,[18] this double and more complex perspective contradicts the traditional separation between natural reality and legal reality, between the living being and the *persona*, between brute and institutional facts. The force of the law is given by the capacity that such a specific socio-legal instrument had to produce the world, to make reality, and those sections of reality which – though not corresponding to natural or brute facts – can also operate performatively on nature and on brute facts. All reality, in this sense, is already (or could be potentially) *legal*. The distinction between facts and norms, following this "technological" and artificial idea of the law, collapses.

The liminal attitude of the law defines borders and describes entities through mechanisms of inclusion and exclusion, and through exceptions: all these mechanisms are aimed at preventing or resolving conflicts and it is for this reason that Roman law would also use the term *lis* to refer to things. The procedure is the *terrain* of emergence of legal reality. Yan Thomas defines this process as the "legal capture" of the world.[19] And still the legal *res*, for Yan Thomas, is not a thing in the common sense, but it corresponds to the operation that qualifies and constitutes the entity, by including it in the legal system.

As noted not only by Thomas, but also in the work of Aldo Schiavone and in particular in *Ius*,[20] Roman jurists would designate, with *res*, all the things that passed through a process of denomination or specification, that needed to enter the taxonomy of legal reality, that were attached to some *causa* and

17 As Giorgio Agamben notes in his preface to *Il valore delle cose*, cit., p. 11 ff.
18 See Giorgio Agamben, preface to *Il valore delle cose*, cit., p. 13.
19 Yan Thomas, *Il valore delle cose*, cit., p. 56.
20 Aldo Schiavone, *Ius. L'invenzione del diritto in Occidente*, Einaudi, Torino, 2005 – especially pp. 193 ff., on formalism and abstraction, and on cases and *res*.

that, thus, reflected a specific interest or value in need for recognition or protection. More than the substance or content of the single *res*-container, it was the procedure of its definition during the dispute originated by the *quaestio disputata* that would recognize an ontological status to the *res*: a procedural ontology was enacted by Roman jurists and commentators.

With a dynamic that has much in common with the "technological" social ontology described by Ferraris, Yan Thomas describes the transformation of the *pecunia publica* into *pecunia sacra* through a deposit into a sacred place (a sanctuary) and a series of other passages. The ritual, or *formula*, was the *tèchne* through which a new status function was attributed to the *pecunia* (*sacramentum*).[21] It was the procedure that allowed the taxonomy. Similarly, in order to create a temple, it was necessary to first sanctify a wood, which then became sacred; and only after that procedure (and *through* that procedure) that very place would have acquired a legal function attributed also by a magistrate. Thomas describes sanctifications and sacralizations as procedures similar to juridifications – where the identification of the place corresponds to the institutionalization of that place into a sacred one.[22]

In Roman law, objects were transformed into legal objects through consecutive specifications, so the distinction between non-legal and legal objects did not exist: it would have been a perspectival error to consider things from the point of view of metaphysics as opposed to those that would belong to the world of physics: *res* were just *res*. Their mode of existence would, instead, depend on the definition of their value.[23] Legal reality was made by a net of different bargains, negotiations, and processes of qualification-evaluation of the things constituting objects of the legal disputes. For this reason, the res would correspond to the price, and this *res* and *pecunia* would define the same socio-legal object.

5. Conclusion: socio-legal reality in the making

Following Thomas, I believe the example of money – as discussed by Searle and Ferraris – and these remarks made on legal res in the Roman world suggest to consider legal reality as a process *in the making*. Entities correspond to an evaluation: a legal object is represented intentionally, must be recorded in order to remain and to be valid, but first and foremost it exists because a negotiation requires an appraisal of a price, of a value at stake – following a judgment done according to the common sense of a specific space and time. This argument is coherent with Maurizio Ferraris's idea of

---

21 Yan Thomas, *Il valore delle cose*, cit., p. 36.
22 Yan Thomas, *Il valore delle cose*, cit., p. 43.
23 Yan Thomas, *Il valore delle cose*, cit., p. 57.

an ontology which cannot do without its technology: it is, indeed, an ontology *in the making* since it is identified with its process of definition. This legal qualification of reality is made through abstractions, and fictions: the status functions described by Searle, in the process of legal qualification of reality, must be recorded in order to exist. As aforementioned, to this extent from the legal perspective the traditional distinction between a dimension of facts and a dimension of norms is just a linguistic distinction with no ontological correspondence. Such an oblique account on legal ontology allows to consider also legal fictions and abstractions as entities composing that mixed physical and metaphysical reality which is legal reality. All derives from the area of conflictuality and of evaluation and balancing of interests which is the core of the production of such a reality. The moment of definition of legal objects through the singular questions posed by the cases qualifies the ontology of the law: the *res* and the *controversia* correspond.[24]

Starting from the comparison between two contemporary philosophers, through a passage in the history of the formation of legal reality, in this chapter I argued that law is a unique practice of construction of the world that surrounds us, a practice which is both performative and documental – and that, actually, the ontology of the law derives from this very practice which is a hybridization of intentionality and documentality.

Some decades before the aforementioned works of Thomas and Schiavone, Italian jurist Santi Romano had written an entry of a legal dictionary on legal reality.[25] Romano describes legal reality as a complex order in permanent formation, where different relations are possible between reality and *legal* reality: the two could be, for instance, independent from each other – there would be, in that case, no collision between the two different realities. Otherwise, the two could be divergent, but not independent from each other. A legal order is made, according to Romano, by norms (complexes of norms), but also by institutions, entities, social bodies – among them there are also abstractions, and sometimes the law makes use of fictions. Both devices are equally important in the construction of legal reality, though in one case there is no correspondence with reality (fiction) and in the other case a foundation in reality is needed (abstraction). Fictions substitute imaginary facts to real facts (both are different from what

---

24 See Marta Madero, "Interpreting the Western Legal Tradition. Reading the Work of Yan Thomas" (2012, transl. by Kathleen Guilloux) 1 Annales, in *Annales. Histoire, Sciences Sociales*, pp. 103–132.

25 Santi Romano, *Frammenti di un dizionario giuridico*, Giuffrè, Milano, 1983, pp. 204 ff (*Realtà giuridica*). Romano's theory of the legal order as an institutional order among other systems of normativity had been developed already in his masterpiece *L'ordinamento giuridico* (1917–1918), now translated by Mariano Croce (*The Legal Order*, Routledge, 2017).

is *really* outside in the world and both exist in the legal realm). From his perspective, both legal fictions and abstractions show that the entities created *ex novo* in the law are not created *ex nihilo*, but they are instead based on a material substrate from which legal reality emerges. Legal reality is definitely different from the substrate itself. For example, people might think that a municipality is a geographical entity on top of which legal language creates the entity "municipality". Romano adds that the creativity of legal language is broad and in fact there are other types of relations between legal reality and the world – which include, for instance, presumptions. These are not fictions – they do not modify reality in any way; and yet, they can produce consequences at the level of legal reality. All these instruments make legal reality; the plurality of such mechanisms is also affirmed by Schiavone in his *Ius*, where he claims that legal sciences originated in the abstraction of social relations into a system of formalized and intangible exchanges, obligations, pretenses, subjects, actions.[26] To each moment of abstraction, a name was attached. Names of legal objects thus reflected the legal substance of the things since there are generated by the need to prevent or resolve conflicts. Names were linked to the use.

Law was, already at the time of Mucius (1st century BCE), the realization of an instrumental rationality related to the evaluation of singular situations and to the realization of exchanges; it was a *social technology* aimed at regulating conflicts and constituted a cognitive barrier through which the world could be approached. Precisely in that period, Schiavone adds, the objects defined through legal language started to constitute a sort of autonomous metaphysics aimed at transforming abstract schemes of social relations into beings: an autonomous ontology.[27] The formalism which constitutes one of the principal characteristics of law was thus a way to establish the existence of things at a level which was intermediate between language and reality. This "thirdness" is exactly what characterizes law as a technology aimed at mediating, following Ferraris, between the ontological and the epistemic dimensions – a thirdness which, by the way, characterized the very emergence of money, the exemplary socio-legal object from which the arguments in this chapter originated. Money substituted barter and brought transactions at a more abstract level. This is very likely why money is among the favorite examples used by Searle and Ferraris to give examples of their arguments: because it has always been a "universal equivalent" of human relations.[28]

---

26 Aldo Schiavone, *Ius. L'invenzione del diritto in Occidente*, cit., pp. 194 ff.

27 Aldo Schiavone, *Ius. L'invenzione del diritto in Occidente*, cit., pp. 196 ff.

28 Aldo Schiavone, *Ius. L'invenzione del diritto in Occidente*, cit., pp. 203–204.

Conclusion

Angela Condello

1. Medium of exchange

By depicting money as a tool or medium of exchange, Simmel describes it as a social phenomenon situated at the intersection between individuals and society. Moreover, he shows how money can be considered as a paradigmatic social object, because all societal structures are constructed on the balance between individuals and society:

> The balance between these two poles is less banal than one might expect, for the two poles are themselves immediately rethematized in the one place in which Simmel's work does take on the appearance of something like a system, namely, in that well-nigh metaphysical opposition between life and form.[1]

Simmel builds a dialectic of objectification: in his theory, exchange and social entities are objectified. Exchange, in his theory, becomes a "third" dimension, in which the mediation between singularities and society takes place. Since money is the material realization of such an exchange and mediation, and in some sense it constitutes its epiphany, then it can be considered as the cornerstone element of all societal equilibria and relations. As a matter of fact, the German intellectual depicts it as *the* fundamental social entity.

Marcel Mauss, in his theory of the gift, had argued that the main function of exchange, in archaic societies, was to produce friendly feelings between people – and if it did not do this, exchange would have failed its main purpose.[2]

---

1 Friedric Jameson, "The Theoretical Hesitation. Benjamin's Sociological Predecessor", in *Critical Inquiry*, Vol. 25, No. 2, "Angelus Novus: Perspectives on Walter Benjamin" (Winter, 1999), pp. 267–288, p. 272.
2 Marcel Mauss, *The Gift: Forms and Functions of Exchange in Archaic Societies*, transl. by Ian Cunnison, Cohen and West, London, 1925, p. 18.

In the same archaic societies, the gift entailed circulation and exchange: a gift received, writes Mauss, is an object owned;[3] but the ownership is of a particular kind: it is both property and possession, a pledge and a loan, an object sold and an object bought, a deposit, a trust; it is given only on condition that it will be used on behalf of, or transmitted to, a third person. Exchange – presented as the basic dynamic on which money functions – is very similar to the circular movement that characterizes the use of gifts as described by Mauss. And, yet, it is also very different.

Simmel, in fact, tries to problematize exchange in order to use its temporality and its procedural nature. For him, "Exchange, i.e. the economy, is the source of economic values, because exchange is the representative of the distance between subject and object which transforms subjective feelings into objective valuation".[4] Exchange is at the core of all societal relations because it represents the space of an evaluation. If there was no need to exchange substances, workforce, powers or rights, then economy would not exist. On the contrary, the reciprocity which is at the core of the constitution of institutions originates in the need to exchange goods, or actions and performances: it originates, in other words, in the need to have something that we do not possess naturally. Thus, it represents the product of an opening movement towards the external world, toward *the other*: an opening movement that requires criteria, guarantees and evaluation. That needs, in other words, to be quantified and evaluated in order to be regulated: hence, the function of money. *Money is what money does*:

> In the economy, this distance is brought about through exchange, through the two-sided influence of barriers, obstacles and renunciation. Economic values are produced by the same reciprocity and relativity that determine the economic character of values.[5]

The thirdness of the exchange is a medium: when two subjects exchange goods, money, or other things, that space of communication between the two is not just an addition of two processes – giving and receiving – but it is a new phenomenon. Both processes are, at the same time, cause and effect of the exchange. Money is a unit of measurement and it measures value: this value develops in the thirdness of the exchange: a regulatory phenomenon that has its own normative force and its own capacity to attribute force and powers to individuals.

3 Marcel Mauss, *The Gift: Forms and Functions of Exchange in Archaic Societies*, cit., p. 22.
4 Georg Simmel, *The Philosophy of Money*, cit., p. 94.
5 Georg Simmel, *The Philosophy of Money*, cit., p. 95.

It is a social institution that informs and regulates the society from which it originates: like law, the function of money shows the reflexivity of society. Money is therefore one of those normative ideas that obey the norms that they represent and contribute to create. Another crucial aspect in Simmel's theory of money that invites us to draw a parallel between money and law – meant as both regulatory social phenomena – is the representation of money as both multiple and infinitely various, on the other hand; and, on the other hand, stable and unified as an expression of value.[6] Friedrich Jameson has noted that money "must obviously be somehow valuable, yet the very conception of the value of its 'substance' tends to project the whole phenomenon of value onto a quite different, nonmonetary plane (something which modern theory has described, following Freudian and Lacanian psychoanalysis, as the exclusion of the material of value from the realm of exchange)".[7]

2. Money (as law) is a social technology

Money is separated from the objects by the fact of exchange. It mediates the exchange of objects. Simmel wrote:[8]

> Money is perhaps the clearest expression and demonstration of the fact that man is a "tool-making" animal, which, however, is itself connected with the fact that man is a "purposive" animal. The concept of means characterizes the position of man in the world; he is not dependent as is an animal upon the mechanism of instinctual life and immediate volition and enjoyment, nor does he have unmediated power, such as we attribute to a god, such that his will is identical with its realization. He stands between the two in so far as he can extend his will far beyond the present moment, but can realize it only in a roundabout way through a teleological series which has several links [. . .]. Means [. . .] and their enhanced form, the tool, symbolize the human genus. The tool illustrates or incorporates the grandeur of the human will, and at the same time its limitations.

Money is a *concrete* instrument which corresponds with its function and with its abstract concept; it is a *pure instrument*. It is so important to

6 Friedric Jameson, "The Theoretical Hesitation. Benjamin's Sociological Predecessor", cit., p. 281.
7 Friedric Jameson, "The Theoretical Hesitation. Benjamin's Sociological Predecessor", cit., p. 283.
8 Georg Simmel, *The Philosophy of Money*, cit., pp. 226–227.

understand society that it can be considered, like law, a paradigmatic social object because it sublimates the relations among men and between men and the objects of their wills: money, as Searle claims, attributes power – first and foremost, the power to act freely and to do what one wants. It is the language that gives content to human relations by measuring them and by attributing value to each transaction, real or symbolic.

Actually, new forms of money such as bitcoin confirm the abstract, dematerialized, recorded, and alienating nature of money. Money, in fact, remains a medium that bridges and – at the same time – creates distance between subjects and objects, by connecting them reciprocally. Even though dematerialized, in order to exist digital money must be recorded: it must reflect a series of data that can be transferred. From the time when money replaced barter, it has been a medium that operates in the space *in between* and that bridges the distance between traders and goods, making it possible to trade also at great distance (in space and time). For the same reason, though, money creates distance, and alienates: "in order to mediate the exchange relation, money has to assume an impersonal, detached form [. . .]. Personal trading relationships are replaced by impersonal exchange".[9] As mentioned at the beginning of this conclusive section, more archaic forms of exchange such as gifts were linked to more personal and less distant relations than those typical of modern societies. And, yet, money must be the product of an abstraction and it must remain impersonal: if it were *a* specific object, it could never balance every single object or be the bridge between different objects. It *is* nothing but the relation between economic values themselves, embodied in a tangible substance.

Its theoretical importance is that it constitutes a symbol, an image of the formula according to which things receive meaning through each other reciprocally, and are determined by their mutual relations.

Abstraction, distance, reciprocity, separation, interconnection, exchange: these are the key words of money (and of law) understood as *social technologies*.

---

9 Georg Simmel, *The Philosophy of Money*, cit., p. 361.

Bibliography

Austin, J.L. (1962), *How to Do Things With Words*, Cambridge, MA: Harvard University Press.

Condello A., Searle, J.R. (2017), "Some Remarks About Social Ontology and Law: An Interview With John R. Searle", in *Ratio Juris*, Vol. 30, No. 2, pp. 226–231.

Condello, A., Searle J.R., Ferraris, M. (2018), "Two Questions on the Ontology of Money. An Imaginary Dialogue Between John Rogers Searle and Maurizio Ferraris", in *Ardeth*, 3/2018, pp. 181–191.

Croce, M. (2018), *The Politics of Juridification*, London: Routledge.

Debray, R. (2001), *Dieu, un itinéraire. Matériaux pour l'histoire de l'Éternel en Occident*, Paris: Odile Jacob.

De Jorio, A. (1832), *La mimica degli antichi investigata nel gestire napoletano*, Napoli: Stamperia del Fibreno, facsimile Sala Bolognese, A. Forni, 2002.

Dennett, D.C. (2017), *From Bacteria to Bach and Back: The Evolution of Minds*, Cambridge, MA: Bradford Books/MIT Press.

Derrida, J. (1968), "La différance", in Id., *Marges de la philosophie*, Paris: ed. de Minuit, 1972.

———. (1971), "Signature, événement, contexte", poi in Id., *Marges de la philosophie*, Paris: ed. de Minuit, 1972.

———. (1988), *Limited Inc.*, Evanston, IL: Northwestern University Press.

De Soto, H. (2000), *The Mystery of Capital: Why Capitalism Triumphs in the West and Fails Everywhere Else*, New York, NY: Basic Books.

Epstein, B. (2015), *The Ant Trap: Rebuilding the Foundations of the Social Sciences*, Oxford: Oxford University Press.

Ferraris, M. (1997), *Estetica razionale*, Milano: Cortina, 2011.

———. (2001), *Il mondo esterno*, Milano: Bompiani.

———. (2004), *Goodbye Kant! What Still Stands of the Critique of Pure Reason*, New York: SUNY Press, 2013.

———. (2005), *Where Are You? Ontology of the Mobile Phone*, New York: Fordham University Press, 2014.

———. (2009), *Documentality. Why It Is Necessary to Leave Traces*, New York: Fordham University Press, 2012.

———. (2014), *Mobilitazione totale*, Roma-Bari: Laterza.

————. (2016), *Emergenza*, Torino: Einaudi.

————. (2017), *Postverità e altri enigmi*, Bologna: il Mulino.

Guala, F. (2016), *Understanding Institutions: The Science and Philosophy of Living Together*, Princeton, NJ: Princeton University Press.

Jameson, F. (1999), "The Theoretical Hesitation. Benjamin's Sociological Predecessor", in *Critical Inquiry*, Vol. 25, No. 2, "Angelus Novus": Perspectives on Walter Benjamin, pp. 267–288.

Lawson, T. (2016), "Social Positioning and the Nature of Money", in *Cambridge Journal of Economics*, Vol. 40, No. 4, pp. 961–996.

McGinn, C. (2015), *Prehension*, Cambridge, MA: The MIT Press.

Maddalena, G. (2015), *The Philosophy of Gesture*, Montreal and London: McGill-Queen's University Press.

Madero, M. (2012), "Interpreting the Western Legal Tradition. Reading the Work of Yan Thomas" (transl. by Kathleen Guilloux), 1 Annales, in *Annales. Histoire, Sciences Sociales*, pp. 103–132.

Marconi, D. (1997), *Lexical Competence*, Cambridge, MA: The MIT Press.

Mauss, M. (1925), *The Gift. Forms and Functions of Exchange in Archaic Societies*, transl. by Ian Cunnison, London: Cohen and West.

Menger, K. (1892), "On the Origin of Money", in *The Economic Journal*, Vol. 2, No. 6. (Jun., 1892), pp. 239–255.

Mulqueen, T., Matthews, D. (2015), *Being Social: Ontology, Law, Politics*, Oxford: Counterpress.

Pareyson, L. (1950), *Estetica. Teoria della formatività*, Milano: Bompiani, 1989.

Pascal, B., *Pensées*, ed. by Léon Brunschvicg.

Romano, S. (1983), *Frammenti di un dizionario giuridico*, Milano: Giuffrè.

Schiavone, A. (2005), *Ius. L'invenzione del diritto in Occidente*, Torino: Einaudi.

Searle, J.R. (1995), *The Construction of Social Reality*, New York: The Free Press.

————. (2010), *Making the Social World: The Structure of Human Civilization*, Oxford: Oxford University Press.

————. (2017), "Money: Ontology and Deception", in *Cambridge Journal of Economics*, Vol. 41, pp. 1453–1470.

Searle, J.R., Ferraris, M. (2018), *Il denaro e i suoi inganni*, ed. and with an essay by A. Condello, Torino: Einaudi.

Searle, J.R., Smith, B. (2003), "The Construction of Social Reality: An Exchange", in *American Journal of Economics and Sociology*, Vol. 6, No. 2.

Sermonti, G. (2009), *L'alfabeto scende dalle stelle. Sull'origine della scrittura*, Milano-Udine: Mimesis.

Simmel, G. (1900), *The Philosophy of Money*, London and New York: Routledge, 2004.

Simondon, G. (1958), *Du mode d'existence des objets techniques*, Paris: Aubier-Montaigne.

Spengler, O. (1918), *Der Untergang des Abendlandes. Umrisse einer Morphologie der Weltgeschichte*, Wien: Verlag Braumüller.

Thomas, Y. (1995), *Fictio legis*, ed. by Michele Spanò and with and essay by M. Spanò and M. Vallerani, Macerata: Quodlibet, 2016.

————. (2002), *Il valore delle cose*, ed. by Michele Spanò and with essays by G. Agamben and M. Spanò, Macerata: Quodlibet, 2015.

Vico, G.B. (1744), "*La scienza nuova*", in *The New Science of Giambattista Vico: Unabridged Translation of the Third Edition (1744) With the Addition of "Practic of the New Science"*, Ithaca: Cornell University Press, 2016.

Warburton, W. (1742), *The Divine Legation of Moses Demonstrated*, ripr. della ed. 1765, New York and London: Garland, 1978.

Zagrebelsky, G. (2012), *Simboli al potere*, Torino: Einaudi.

Index

Printed in the United States
by Baker & Taylor Publisher Services